SAFARI PRESS

A Quail Hunter's Odyssey

The author with Hannah.

A Quail Hunter's Odyssey

by

Dr. Joseph C. Greenfield Jr.

Forewords

by

Jim Rikhoff and Joey O'Bannon

Safari Press

Greenfield, Dr. Joseph C., Jr

First Safari Press edition

Safari Press
2009 Long Beach, California

ISBN 1-57157-336-4

Library of Congress Catalog Card Number: 2008933272

10 9 8 7 6 5 4 3 2 1

Printed in China

This book is dedicated with a deep sense of gratitude to a number of pointers and one setter that have owned me for the past half-century. I am deeply indebted to them for providing a lifetime of pleasure. Also, I must salute the other player, the bobwhite quail, a true gentleman, whose unwilling participation made these adventures possible.

Table of Contents

Foreword

Someone once remarked that "while he wouldn't go to hell to hunt quail, he'd probably hang around the edge until he fell in." I can certainly identify with those sentiments and, I suspect, Dr. Joseph Greenfield—Joe to his hunting buddies—would heartily endorse our position. There have been a lot of words lavished on Mr. Robert Quail—Yes, he is a gentleman and sometimes deserves a formal address—so it would seem somewhat pointless to add to the volumes already devoted to that splendid game bird.

Well, I can certainly attest to the fact that we would be wrong to come to such a conclusion. I have read just about everything that has been printed about quail—at least the good stuff—and I am both pleased and surprised to find that Joe Greenfield has indeed not only added to the lore of the bobwhite, but that contribution has also been significant and well-written. Dr. Greenfield is truly a Renaissance man, and his accomplishments in the medical and sporting fields have been outstanding.

Dr. Greenfield first contacted me in March 2000 through an agent (with whom we quickly dispensed; after all, who needs an intermediary between two such open-minded, kindly, and gentle birdhunters!). In no time flat, we were carrying on a conversation by both telephone and mail.

As it happens, I have a background that—in some ways—is similar to the Doctor's. He had a great-grandfather who was a surgeon in the Army of Northern Virginia, while I had a great-great grandfather who was a surgeon in an Alabama regiment, who later became a medical missionary in the Balkans after the Civil War. I have hunted all my life—and I am two months older than he—and those seventy-two years have not been wasted by either of us. We both have kept our priorities straight and have never let extraneous things get in the way of quail hunting and good bird dogs.

Now, as always must happen, there we have come to a gentle parting of the ways. Joe is a zealous—fanatical?—devotee of pointers. I, being of a more sensitive nature, have always been an English-setter man. We do agree, however, that Brittany spaniels, while nice little fellows, are, after all, "Frog Dogs." Nonetheless, it has been my experience that a lot of pointers are what I call "advertising dogs"—put them down in one county and advertise for 'em in the next! Seriously, since Dr. Greenfield admits to owning one good setter, I, too, can attest that I have seen some fine pointers . . . just never wanted to own one.

Make no mistake, 'tho, Joe Greenfield knows his dogs, and his chapters on them will teach every (may I say it?) old dog new tricks. In fact, you can pretty well be sure that if there is something important you should know about pointing dogs, you will find it in this book, for it is a volume as much about bird dogs as it is about bobwhite quail. You should remind yourself that Joe used the term pointers in two senses: First, generally, in that what he writes may be applied to all the pointing breeds, and secondly, specifically, as he sees most things through the eyes of a man conditioned to running American (or English) pointers almost exclusively.

Dr. Greenfield then takes you on a thoughtful evaluation of what used to be quail hunting (and I can remember the pre-war South and just after the Second World War) and what it is today, and where it is going. When I consider the future of quail hunting, as with most of the field sports, I am glad I lived when I did. I do not hold much hope for future generations, unless the sports they enjoy are golf, skiing, boating, and other exercises.

I have not dwelt on Dr. Greenfield's incredible medical experience, but you can be assured of the fact that his career has been one of the most outstanding in American medicine, culminating in his being appointed chairman of the Department of Medicine at Duke University Medical Center. I could easily spend another two pages outlining his accomplishments, but I think both he and the reader would rather follow a good dog into quail country. Be my guest . . . you will be fully entertained.

Jim Rikhoff
Speakeasy Hill
High Bridge, New Jersey
July 15, 2003

Foreword to the Revised Edition

The publication of this revised edition occurs at the time of a major milestone: Doc and I have been quail (bird) hunting together for twenty-five years. I vividly remember seeing him for the first time. I had just finished a job as a cowboy running a feedlot and decided to try my hand at running a quail-hunting preserve. He arrived late in the season with two female bird dogs, Tiny and Hannah. The first was a hard-hunting, effervescent little pointer. The other pointer, while a very good bird dog, did her best to aggravate the "living hell" out of Doc.

On our first hunt together, I remember him dropping a high-grade Parker double-barrel shotgun on the ground in order to admonish Hannah for refusing to hunt for dead birds. He turned so red-faced that I thought he was going to have a stroke right then and there.

For reasons that have never been completely clear, we quickly developed a warm and lasting friendship. To characterize him as opinionated is somewhat of an understatement. (Luckily, I share the majority of his dogmatic beliefs.) He and I have hunted birds together at least five weeks each year since that time. Although from vastly different backgrounds, Doc and I share a common passion—hunting quail with English pointer bird dogs, which transcends all of our differences.

For the past quarter century, we've gone through a number of ups and downs while hunting in a variety of locations in Florida and have trained a "truckload" of pointer bird dogs. In addition, for several years we've hunted Sage grouse in Wyoming and have been on ten safaris to Africa to hunt dangerous game. But, without a doubt, our experiences bird hunting together have been, by far, the most memorable. On too many occasions, we have had the heart-rending experience of watching a superb pointer grow old. However, at least so far, we have been able to train first-class replacements and continue the pursuit of bobwhite quail. As a matter of fact, our current group of pointers, in my opinion, are among our best.

I have hunted with lots of different people in the past twenty-five years as a professional guide. The thing that stands out about Doc more than anyone else is his passion for good pointer bird dogs. Ninety-eight percent of bird hunters today talk about their guns or how many birds they shot or what a great shot they made. Doc doesn't give a damn about any of that. It's all about his love for hunting quail with English pointers. (We share the same passion for bird dogs.) He shoots a Purdey and can effectively kill quail. But when he speaks of hunting quail, it's all about his bird dogs. You would think to listen to him that he loves his pointers better than either people or medicine. (I believe he does!)

For me, hunting with Doc is different. The majority of my quail hunting is with clients, where I act as a guide. With him, it's simply the two of us bird hunting together, joking with each other, and enjoying the pointers' performance—and as a secondary component, killing quail. In the past few years, both of us have developed a significant problem with our hearing, but other than that, we are able to partake to the fullest extent the pleasures of hunting bobwhite quail. It has been my honor to have known and hunted with Doc and to call him my friend. As Doc has expressed on a number of occasions, "I hope this odyssey never ends."

Joey O'Bannon
J&R Outfitters
Indiantown, FL
May 2008

Acknowledgments

In the body of the text, I have acknowledged the multiple friends with whom I have hunted over the years and to whom I am deeply indebted. However, one individual deserves special recognition: Joey O'Bannon. For more than twenty-five years he has been largely responsible for the exceptional quail-hunting experiences that I have had in Florida.

William Hoffman helped to alter my pedantic-scientific style of writing.

William Jarrett played an instrumental role in bringing this manuscript to publication.

Judith C. Rembert not only carefully edited the text, but also provided advice regarding both the content and style of the work.

Bettie C. Houston willingly prepared multiple revisions of the manuscript.

Lesa M. Hall rejuvenated many of the photographs.

Will McIntyre of Winston-Salem, North Carolina, gave permission to use the frontispiece photograph.

I am extraordinarily grateful to many of my colleagues for their encouragement during the preparation of this book.

The obvious professionalism and expertise of Monica Sullivan has markedly enhanced the presentation of these musings. Without the support and inspiration provided by Jim Rikhoff, there would be no book.

Both Ludo Wurfbain and Jacque Neufeld were instrumental in bringing forth this revised edition.

Introduction

"Frankly, I Don't Give a Damn." My purpose in writing this book has been to document my experiences hunting birds, specifically eastern bobwhite quail *(Colinus virginianus)*, over a span of sixty years. In this quest, I have walked and/or ridden tens of thousands of miles and have seen the changes that have occurred in bird hunting—none of them for the best. The sport has been transformed from a fairly ubiquitous pastime available to almost everyone to the current situation where hunting wild quail is either essentially nonexistent or extraordinarily expensive.

Throughout this time I've occasionally strayed from the role of single-species bird hunter to hunting other game, including rabbit, to which I am grateful for providing my first opportunity to hunt with dogs; fox, for two or three years, which I very much enjoyed; deer, about as exciting as shooting a Guernsey cow in a barn; turkey—I never mastered imitating a lovesick hen; squirrel, I still hunt two or three times a year, mainly because I enjoy shooting a .22 rifle; woodcock, a mediocre substitute for quail; dove and snipe, sporty shooting, but a major minus is the absence of pointers; sage grouse, a welcome change for the pointers and myself; pheasant, a creature totally devoid of class; duck and goose—too much sitting, waiting, and freezing. For the past several years I've enjoyed hunting dangerous game in Africa, but that is another tale.

Chapters II–V describe my hunting experiences generally in chronological order in various geographic sections of the South. The rest of the book details, in a somewhat haphazard fashion, the many facets of the sport of quail hunting. The reader will soon determine that, as a bird hunter, I appear to be self-assured, opinionated, and intolerant of the approaches taken by others. All true! Still, I don't claim to know everything about bird hunting—not by a long shot—but I have had a wide and varied set of experiences, and I've gained a modicum of understanding about the sport.

During the past five years, the lathe of time has continued to turn. I must thank a Kind Providence for affording me the opportunity to continue my odyssey in the pursuit of bobwhite quail. The Florida venue has been ideal. Although three of my closest companions, Faith, Jeb, and Humphrey are no longer alive, several new additions have stepped up to the plate and are hitting home runs. In this revised edition, the Florida chapter has undergone a significant update. In addition, there are six new chapters. The last chapter attempts to put into perspective what my odyssey has been all about.

Writing this book from voluminous contemporary notes has allowed me to relive many cherished hours spent afield. Everything described contains at least a grain of truth, though I confess that nothing has "lost any fat in the telling." Whether this book is read or appreciated by anyone else is of no particular moment to me. "Frankly, I don't give a damn."

The Beginning

Chapter I

I was about ten years old when I first hunted birds. For the previous two years, I had hunted squirrels—my father having taught me how to shoot a .22 rifle—but I had never seen a bird dog in action.

My father, an excellent pistol shot who rarely hunted, had been invited to hunt quail near Leesburg, Georgia, and he took me along. Our host, Mr. Charlie Gardner, a bachelor and true Southern gentleman, had spent much of his life bird hunting. His 16-gauge Parker had been fired so often that the tubes (barrels) were worn paper-thin.

The plantation belonged to Mr. Gardner's family but had seen better times. Sharecroppers farmed a portion of the land, each family maintaining a cotton patch (one or two acres) and a vegetable garden. The rest consisted of unused fields and pine woods that were burned at least every other year, a management practice assuring the presence of plenty of feed, cover, and edges—in short, ideal quail habitat one can only dream about today.

Mr. Gardner's plantation featured a "world of birds" that only he hunted. In the past he'd owned many fine bird dogs, but on this occasion the kennel contained just two pointers. I don't remember much about the older dog, but the younger, Lucy, may be described—if one chooses to be generous—as "started."

Lucy ran up and chased covey after covey, and our host spent most of his time cursing and yelling at her. It seemed that the appropriate name for a bird dog was "son-of-a-bitch," a phrase I've found useful on many subsequent occasions to identify obstreperous pointers. After many aggravating episodes, Lucy finally tired of chasing birds and actually pointed.

"Take this shotgun," my father said, handing me his father's 20-gauge Parker. "Try to kill this bird."

A bird flushed, flew over my left shoulder toward the sun, and I still remember seeing the bird in flight and squeezing the trigger. The quail crumpled, whether dying from my shot or Mr. Gardner's, I will never know. This I do know: From that time on I was "ruined." I had found my lifelong pastime.

My father didn't let me shoot any more on this trip, so I went home 100 percent successful as a bird shooter. More important, my mind often replays the excitement of shooting my first bird; thus, I know exactly the day this sport hooked me. I am sure my father's being along undoubtedly contributed to the pull that bird hunting has exerted on me. These are truisms: No one ever makes turkey dressing better than your mother, and no time is more memorable than that spent with your father.

About a year later my father and I hunted near Newnan, Georgia, with a colleague of his in the banking business. On a cold, wet, dreary day we walked from sunrise to sundown and found only one small covey, which flushed and flew away apparently unhurt. The dog pointed a tight-sticking single (a quail that didn't fly off). My father, thinking he had wounded the bird, reached down to pick it up. At that instant, the quail fled the environs unhurt. We went home empty-handed.

My father and I went bird hunting on just one other occasion before he became unable to walk without using a cane following a 1946 automobile accident. On this trip we went to Fitzgerald, Georgia, and, in retrospect, I realize I saw some exceptional dog work—three pointers trailing a covey for approximately one hundred yards. At that time I knew so little about bird dogs I didn't appreciate the impressive sight I had witnessed.

At age thirteen or fourteen, I took a detour from bird hunting and began serious rabbit hunting with beagles. Often, while looking for rabbits, we flushed quail, and I shot at a few with limited success. I used a .22-410 Stevens over-and-under (fine for rabbits, not for birds) my Uncle Paul Greenfield had given me. Later I carried the 20-gauge Parker, much to my father's horror. He thought it a "travesty" to shoot rabbits with this high-grade bird gun.

Through money earned from a paper route and a few shrewd trades, I acquired a pack of five or six excellent beagles. I enjoyed rabbit hunting, especially listening to the dogs run. "Breathes there a man with soul so dead" who wouldn't enjoy the "music" from a pack of hounds?

Mr. Don Williamson of Monroe, Georgia, introduced me to beagle field trials. Initially I participated and had success in two-couple-pack stakes, an event where four rabbit dogs hunt together as a pack to compete effectively. Speed and drive were highly prized characteristics.

Next I entered the standard sanctioned beagle field trial. Here spectators found and jumped the rabbit; then a brace of dogs was released. The dogs were judged primarily on their ability to meticulously follow the trail or "line." Since speed didn't count as a prized attribute, a winning dog could be so slow that the rabbit had time to birth a litter while waiting for the dog to catch up! Because jumping the rabbit didn't count in the scoring, a field trial winner, when actually rabbit hunting, might know no better than to trot around waiting for someone to find the rabbit and to yell, "Tally Ho"—an unlikely event.

To win the standard field trials, I acquired dogs possessing the aforementioned characteristics. Unfortunately, I wound up with beagles that not only had no interest in finding and jumping but might require a day to run a rabbit from one weed patch to another—in essence, worthless as hunters. This entire experience left a long-lasting sour taste in my mouth for field trials.

In spite of my fondness for rabbit hunting, I continuously found myself remembering my first encounter with quail. I could close my eyes and see Lucy pointing, the bird flushing. . . . So at age seventeen, when I had the opportunity to hunt birds in South Georgia with my Uncle Hal, I jumped at the chance.

The South Georgia Years 1948–1955

Chapter II

In 1948, I began bird hunting in earnest with my uncle, Hal Lindsey, who had leased the bird-hunting rights to a tract of land between Cairo and Thomasville, Georgia. Part of these three thousand acres had been planted in corn and soybeans, with the majority in open pine woods used primarily by hogs, scrub cattle, and quail. Located across a road from the lavish Greenwood Plantation, which I had been told was owned by the wealthy Whitney family of New York, the farm we hunted literally teemed with birds. Undoubtedly, one reason for the burgeoning quail population was the fact that many of the Yankee-owned birds flew across the road to feed. In a normal day we found eight to twelve coveys—numbers that are incomprehensible today.

Uncle Hal, a 275-pound Atlanta lawyer who loved hunting and eating, had purchased two pointers, Lemon and Mack, from a man in Griffin, Georgia. This man made a living grinding corn used for mash by local moonshiners, and since grinding corn required just one day a week (for him, the day was Sunday), he spent the remainder of his time hunting birds and training bird dogs. Since Georgia made it illegal to hunt on Sunday (the sense of this law has always escaped me), his apportionment of labor devoted to revenue producing and hunting seemed reasonable.

When first purchased, Lemon and Mack were outstanding, well-trained dogs. Mack, the older, never significantly deteriorated. Lemon, younger and more aggressive, was not disciplined by my uncle and became somewhat uncontrollable, not overly staunch, and an unreliable backer. Lemon, to his credit, nonetheless found a large number of birds.

Uncle Hal also owned two English setters, which he called "puppies," though they were four years old. They were totally worthless animals, except for training me how to pick cockleburs out of their coats. (Undoubtedly, my longtime dislike of setters stems from dealing with these dolts.) But quickly I learned not to complain. My uncle was devoted to them.

During quail season, we hunted on the average of every other week. The standard scenario had me driving his station wagon Friday afternoons from Atlanta and arriving in Thomasville in time for supper. For reasons never clear to me, Uncle Hal felt that the dogs should ride inside the station wagon, not in a trailer. He fed them cheese, fresh eggs, and choice meat—a better diet than mine. As a result, they passed volumes of gas so pungent that even an automatic function like breathing became difficult. In the future, I promised myself that if I had the money, I would buy either a pickup truck equipped with a dog box or pull a dog trailer . . . anything but ride in a closed vehicle with flatulent bird dogs!

Despite their gourmet diet, the dogs, while hunting, enjoyed sampling available offal. One day Mack so infuriated Uncle Hal by ingesting mule droppings that he became nearly apoplectic, hitting the dog with his shotgun (Winchester Deluxe Model 21), breaking the stock, and shouting, "Damn you, I feed you steak and you eat s--t."

I pretended not to see this hilarious drama, but I nearly fainted from holding my breath to keep from laughing. Also, I learned a good lesson—not to become too concerned when my own dogs gulped down something humans consider disgusting.

Uncle Hal and I stayed at the Three Toms' Inn in Thomasville, a fine hotel built around the turn of the twentieth century for rich Northerners who came south to hunt birds. The Three Toms' Inn featured excellent accommodations and food, but on Saturdays, when we awoke at 7:30 A.M., we went elsewhere for breakfast—a nearby greasy spoon where the sole attraction, near as I could tell, was a pretty red-haired waitress. I'm certain my uncle enjoyed watching her behind more than the backsides of the bird dogs. We always lingered at least an hour, never starting to hunt before 9:30 A.M.

I have heard and read that quail arise late in the morning and, thus, only the uninitiated look for them early. Uncle Hal subscribed to this dubious concept, but he didn't fool me: the waitress's rear-end caused us to run late.

Uncle Hal and I hunted until noon. After he took a two-hour nap in the station wagon, we returned to the fields, hunting until dark. We ate at Three Toms' Inn, got a good night's sleep, and drove home leisurely on Sunday. I fervently wished we would start hunting at daylight and not stop until dark, but I wisely tolerated this schedule and his other quirks. After all, Uncle Hal provided me with the best bird hunting I would ever experience.

My uncle's business colleagues occasionally hunted with us. I won't forget one particular day with Albert Loeb, who played football at Georgia Tech during the tenure of the legendary Coach Heisman, for whom the famous trophy is named. Mr. Loeb brought along a black-and-white pointer named Jack. Uncle Hal's demeanor changed the moment he saw the dog.

These two "friends" spent the entire trip to Thomasville grandiosely extolling (lying about) the exploits of their respective bird dogs. I hadn't been exposed to this competitive aspect of bird hunting, but actually the two were merely warming up. The atmosphere really chilled the next morning when we turned out all three dogs—Lemon, Mack, and Jack—at the same time.

The first covey flushed wild, which coveys will sometimes do, but Uncle Hal blamed Jack, showering the animal with verbal abuse. A few minutes later Lemon assumed a stylish point that produced only a stink bird (grass sparrow), which prompted Mr. Loeb to observe slyly, "Quail in South Georgia are becoming much smaller."

Uncle Hal's face flushed red (he hated anyone bad-mouthing his dogs) and mumbled something about the former football player's ancestry. For a moment I feared these two "friends" would come to blows.

Matters worsened. About a hundred yards away I spotted a black-and-white calf, an object the nearsighted Mr. Loeb mistook for his bird dog, exclaiming, "Jack's got 'em."

"Maybe," said Uncle Hal, "we should stop and milk Jack."

"You shouldn't poke fun at other people's infirmities," said Mr. Loeb, feigning deep sensitivity.

And so it went for the rest of the day, a constant jawing about the inadequacies of the dogs. Although we found plenty of birds, the much-maligned pointers, perhaps affected by the criticism, did indeed turn in markedly sub-par performances. Sundown came as a relief (usually I wanted to hunt 'till dark).

The trip's only saving grace was the fact that the two were such poor shots they didn't try to compete as marksmen. When, a year later, Mr. Loeb joined my uncle for another hunt, I suddenly remembered the necessity to write a "long-overdue term paper."

A pair of valuable truisms came from an otherwise unpleasant experience: One, never brag about your bird dog—at least until the hunt is over—for he'll make you a liar every time, and, two, competitive "friends" should not hunt birds together.

To return to bird hunting: Frequently there were glorious, made-in-heaven days when birds seemed to be everywhere. Many times I saw dogs point a covey in a soybean field, and when the birds flushed, several other coveys feeding in the same field joined them in flight. Generally, we didn't follow single birds. Most of them flew into dense, swampy areas, the home of cottonmouth water moccasins, snakes my uncle greatly feared. Hunting single birds made little sense during those halcyon days. Coveys were plentiful.

I remember vividly one bevy that wintered near an old home place surrounded by large live-oak trees that supplied the birds with a hearty acorn diet. This covey contained at least twenty-five quail, and I found them every time I hunted the area, though I made sure never to reduce their numbers significantly.

Although my father was not physically able to accompany me on these hunting escapades with Uncle Hal, he always wanted to hear the complete details of our trips. We discussed many aspects of bird hunting until his death in 1951.

At age twenty, I purchased Spot, my first bird dog, from the same man who sold Lemon and Mack to my uncle. A major setback had befallen Spot's owner (namely, a federal anti-moonshine campaign had forced most of his bootlegger customers out of business). To make ends meet, he was forced to sell two of his trained bird dogs, Spot and a drop.

A business associate of my uncle had first choice, and the gods truly smiled on me when he selected the drop. Although broke, the drop turned out to be a mediocre performer. I paid two hundred dollars for Spot, at that time an enormous sum of money for a bird dog, but today twenty-five times that amount wouldn't touch a dog of his abilities. Anyone could see, right from the start, that the three-year-old Spot knew a lot more about bird hunting than I did. In essence, he trained me.

In late September 1951 I started exercising Spot near Emory University (where I was taking premed courses), an area I knew quite well. As a Cub Scout I'd caught frogs, lizards, and later hunted rabbits on this bottomland. Suddenly, Spot began making (smelling) game and froze. I flushed the covey, proud as I could be, knowing I owned a topnotch bird dog.

During that season I continued hunting with Uncle Hal in Thomasville, but also I had access to a significant amount of land near Fayetteville, Georgia, although I didn't find many birds there. In addition, I hunted in middle Georgia near Macon; in South Georgia around Valdosta, Camilla, and Pelham; and once in Hurtsburg, Alabama. Birds were reasonably plentiful at all these locations, but none matched the numbers on the land my uncle leased near Thomasville.

I kept beagles for the next year and tried to hunt both rabbits and birds. But after I entered Emory University Medical School in 1952, hunting time became scarce. I sold the beagles in order to ration rare recreation hours for bird hunting.

I traded my '39 Chevrolet for a '50 Ford, and one of my cousins built a dog trailer with three compartments. The compartment in front held food and supplies, while the two in back—separated by one-inch heavy plywood—were reserved for the dogs.

Uncle Hal let me hunt without him on the Thomasville lease, with the proviso that I take no one along. I adhered strictly to his wishes and am glad I did because I learned how very enjoyable bird hunting can be when done by one's self. It's the approach I still prefer.

I became acquainted with Mr. Otis Brenson, a bird-dog trainer who lived about ten miles from my uncle's lease in Ochlocknee, Georgia, (a town that achieved national fame as a speed trap). Mr. Brenson, a superb shot, used a short-barrel 20-gauge Winchester Model 12, which, interestingly enough, found its way into my hands forty years later through his physician, a friend of mine.

Late in 1951, Uncle Hal commissioned Mr. Brenson to school his setters, but after a brief trial (and being an honest man), Mr. Brenson said, "The dogs should be killed and trainable replacements found." This assessment made my uncle mad as hell, and he broke off all contact with Mr. Brenson. Stubbornly, he continued hunting the two setters with the same poor results.

In 1953, I purchased Don, a two-year-old dog with minimal training on birds. Don had been allowed to run loose and developed a propensity for rabbit hunting. Mr. Brenson "tuned him up" to eschew rabbits, but Don never really overcame his tendency to hunt in swamps and overgrown bottom fields. He didn't find nearly as many birds as Spot, but he nonetheless ranked as a solid bird dog with a spectacular style of running—a gentle, rolling, effortless gait that covered a lot of ground. He could run from dawn to dark and never tire, a creature of beauty in motion.

Spot had a driving gait—knocking down weeds, cornstalks, small pine trees, and anything else that got in his way. He couldn't keep up with Don, however, on an all-day hunt. When five years old, Spot cut his right front ankle and severed several tendons while traversing a refuse pile containing tin cans. Though the wound readily healed, his toes splayed out, causing him to limp slightly. Regardless, he truly was a bird-finding marvel who used his brains as well as his senses.

Spot was a delight to watch, circling the borders of fields, crisscrossing them a couple of times (no bird could hide from him), then heading to the woods, hunting ten or fifteen yards from the edge. He could cover a ten-acre field in this manner in ten minutes, and if he came back, I could be absolutely certain there were no birds nearby. If he didn't come back, I could be just as sure that he was on point and would stay there until sundown, if necessary.

When I hunted alone in Thomasville, I routinely left Atlanta at 2:00 A.M. on Saturday and began looking for birds at daylight. I didn't quit until dark, and then headed for home. I have no idea of the number of lonely miles driven, pulling the dog trailer. One Christmas Eve, I saw only two cars on the road the entire trip back home to Atlanta.

When I had longer periods of time to hunt, I spent the night with my maternal grandmother in Tallahassee, thirty miles from Thomasville. Highway 319, linking the two cities, sliced through some of the nation's most beautiful bird-hunting venues, plantations one after another dedicated entirely to quail management. Early in the morning, wagons pulled by white mules and packed with overdressed nimrods getting ready to bird hunt were in evidence all along the road.

Truly the best hunting of my life occurred during Christmas vacation, 1953, in Thomasville, and it lasted for a wonderful two weeks. Spot, Don, and I found literally hundreds of birds, though we didn't kill more than ten or twelve a day.

I continued to shoot my grandfather's 20-gauge Parker with good success. In high school I had been captain of our championship rifle team, but I had no formal coaching in the very different sport of wingshooting: A rifle is aimed; a shotgun is pointed.

Don and Spot were real meat dogs and, for pointers, excellent at retrieving. One time I shot at a covey flushing from the other side of a five-foot-high hog-wire fence. I killed two of them and then watched as the dogs cleared the fence almost simultaneously, each one returning with a bird in his mouth.

I vividly remember seeing Spot suddenly point while retrieving a dead bird. I'd never seen a dog point with a bird in his mouth and still can't understand how any dog could smell another bird with the overwhelming scent of a dead one filling his nostrils.

Spot never ceased to amaze me. Once, while jumping a fence, he stiffened in mid-air and landed in a classic point. Apparently, he had smelled the birds only after becoming airborne, and though he landed in the middle of the huddled bevy, they didn't flush.

As noted, the fences stood about five feet high and usually consisted of hog wire with two strands of barbed wire on top. One of Spot's failings involved never learning to climb over or crawl under fences. He simply jumped over them. Interestingly, I kept him behind a five-foot fence his entire life, and he never jumped out. In contrast, when hunting he would sail over anything!

Spot's approach to fences worked fine until he reached age eight or nine and began catching his back legs on the barbed wire. I couldn't break him of the habit and numerous times had to extract him from a fence. I always carried sutures to sew up the cuts on his legs.

There was only one drawback with Spot and Don: Though bird hunting comprised their Number One enjoyment in life, fighting with each other didn't lag far behind. It is a continuing mystery to me how male pointers can hunt as a team all day without any semblance of friction or discord, but when the hunt is over—either at lunchtime or sundown—they immediately try to tear each other apart. On one occasion, while traveling, they nearly chewed through a one-inch-thick plywood partition in the dog trailer trying to get at each other.

Spot and Don were always ready to mix it up with local "house dogs," regardless of size, that happened upon us, but they always seemed to lose these fights, returning in various stages of disrepair.

Spot and Don, moderately wide-ranging dogs, covered large chunks of ground, but I could count on them to check back with me regularly. I learned to walk at a reasonable pace and let them do the bulk of the work. I have hunted with people who seem to believe that the main purpose of bird hunting is to see how fast they can walk, and although they are skilled bird hunters, they primarily hurry from one place to another where they know a covey is located. The truth is, the only dog they need is a retriever.

Because Spot and Don possessed so much talent, I didn't learn as much as I should have about the intricacies of bird hunting. I simply followed their lead, enjoying the solitude and the outdoors. Undoubtedly, I developed an over-inflated idea of my prowess as a bird hunter. For example, the deleterious effects of weather conditions—temperature, humidity, direction and speed of the wind—largely escaped me. Later, I learned how these factors dramatically affect a hunter's ability to find birds (and how to use them as excuses for a poor day).

Like most hunters, I became convinced that bird hunting was chiefly a waste of time until two hours before sundown. On several occasions, however, this rule proved not to be correct. I remember hunting one morning with Uncle Hal without much success. While he took his two-hour, midday siesta, Spot, Don, and I worked an area of fairly open pine wood where we had found a few birds in the past.

A light rain was falling, and in just ninety minutes we discovered six or seven coveys. I shot sparingly, not wanting to make Uncle Hal mad by waking him. Most of the time, when I saw the dogs on point, I sat down, watched for a while, and then flushed the birds without shooting. Spot didn't appreciate this approach. He rolled his eyes and gave me a "what-in-the-world-are-you-doing?" look.

The significant effect of moisture on scenting conditions did not ring a bell with me, but I couldn't miss noticing that I had less luck with very wet or bone-dry ground. An obvious factor negatively impacting bird hunting was wind. Once I hunted an entire day with a 20-MPH wind blowing from the northeast, and I found only one covey, which I saw on the road, but the dogs couldn't scent it.

The hogs that lived in the piney woods gave me little trouble, although occasionally I was treed by a mad sow with young pigs. The scrub cattle, however, were a different kettle of fish. These semiwild creatures took pleasure in chasing me, disrupting the work of my dogs, and, in general, making a nuisance of themselves. (They looked so run-down and tough that I couldn't picture anyone eating them. I suspected a fork couldn't penetrate gravy made from even a choice cut.) In fact, I was quite certain that if Heaven were cracked up to what it was supposed to be, there would be no cows. (Only when I began hunting in Florida did I realize the positive qualities on quail management provided by cattle. They keep vegetation thinned, so the birds have a place to run.)

During these years, Georgia was an open-range state, meaning cows, pigs, mules—livestock in general—didn't have to be fenced. Several times while driving at night, I came close to meeting my Maker because these animals congregated on highways after dark, presumably basking in the sun's warmth that radiated from the pavement.

Most of the fallow land in South Georgia was burned each year in winter or early spring, which prevented vegetation from growing so thick it choked out the bird habitat.

Predator control constituted a standard part of every farmer's life. Chickens, guineas, turkeys and, domestic ducks all ran loose near the farmhouse. Protecting them from hawks, owls, foxes, snakes, opossums and raccoons was all part of the day's work. In fact, many farmers, especially during the Depression, considered raccoons and opossums to be acceptable table fare.

The practice of eliminating, without quarter, these predators undoubtedly aided the quail population. Herbert L. Stoddard's research *(The Bob White Quail, Its Habits, Preservation and Increase)* found that just two species of hawks, Cooper's and Sharp-shinned, posed a threat to the propagation of quail. Nevertheless, the overwhelming majority of the local gentry assumed all hawks were "chicken hawks," the enemy, and acted accordingly.

Diamondback rattlesnakes populated the Thomasville area hunting ground, but I encountered surprisingly few. One time I suspected by the way Spot pointed (looking down and drawing back) that he had found something quite different. I saw the snake, heard its ominous rattle and shot it before any harm could be done. A veterinarian from Thomasville told me one of his clients had lost three dogs in as many days to rattlesnake bites. These imported dogs had no experience with snakes and, apparently, lacked an innate fear of them.

Between 1952–54, I hunted almost exclusively with Spot and Don. Then, in 1954, I purchased a puppy sired by Paladin, a national champion, and the dog ultimately grew into a powerhouse. Before I completed his training, however, my bird hunting was significantly curtailed by moving to North Carolina, for internship at Duke Medical Center in 1956.

My mother kept the dogs, bless her heart, but three were too many for her to handle, and I had to divest myself of Don and the puppy. The man who bought them got one hell of a deal. I kept Spot until he died in 1963.

Like so many times in life, I didn't appreciate a wonderful situation until it had ended. Clearly, during this period, bird hunting of unmatched quality existed in the South. I fervently wish I could enjoy similar experiences—even just once—today.

My First

How I got Spot is quite a tale.
His bird hunter owner got sent to jail.
The crime involved a bootlegging deal;
Each Sunday he spent grinding meal.
Six days a week, come rain or shine,
Spot hunted quail in Georgia's pine.
When I bought My First at the age of three,
He'd found and pointed many a covey.
He'd run the edges with tireless speed
To catch the scent as quail moved to feed.
No wasted motion on barren ground;
Spot knew where birds would be found.
What Spot thought of me I can only guess:
A "make out" hunter or just a pest.
Patiently he showed me all the ropes
With coveys and singles how to cope.
Near fifty years have faded into night
Since Spot taught me how to hunt Bobwhite.
Though many others have hunted with me,
My First is frozen in memory.
(1998)

The Middle Georgia Years 1954–1964

Chapter III

In 1954, I started hunting in Bleckley County—having obtained access through my family to a number of farms consisting of small fields containing cotton, soybeans, corn, and peanuts. Most of the farmers raised hogs and a few cattle and fenced the crop fields with hog wire topped by barbed wire to allow the livestock to fatten on unharvested corn and peanuts. Frequently, there was a pair of fences separated by ten or twelve feet, so the livestock could be driven between two fields.

These fencerows made ideal cover for birds, and some of the cattle pastures were planted in Bahia grass that contains a seed desired by quail. When I first started hunting, a significant amount of farmland had been removed from crop production and planted in young pine trees through the auspices of a federal soil bank program. This fallow land, covered with weeds, beggar's lice, lespedeza, etc., made ideal bird habitat.

Unfortunately, over the ensuing eight to ten years, the pine trees grew and crowded out the ground vegetation, destroying the small game cover. Moreover, farming practices also changed dramatically. Cultivating much larger fields without edges—clean farming—resulted in a marked degradation of habitat. In addition, the practice of clean farming forced most of the tenants to leave, and with them disappeared the small gardens, pea patches, and the constant war on predators.

Before all this took place in middle Georgia, I could count on finding four to six coveys a day, not as many as in South Georgia, but certainly adequate.

Something much more detrimental to my bird hunting enjoyment occurred in 1956 when I moved to Durham, North Carolina, to begin my house staff training at Duke Medical Center. Subsequently, I found myself in Bethesda, Maryland, for military service at the National Heart Institute (both together took six years). Through all of this I could squeeze only two weeks of hunting into each year. If I had to do it all over again, from my current perspective, I'd stay in Atlanta and concentrate more on bird hunting than becoming a physician.

I really did miss bird hunting—the feel of a good double shotgun, the pointers, the birds—all enjoyed in solitude. Bird hunting had become more than a hobby for me. It was a passion. I loved everything about the sport.

Initially, in middle Georgia, I hunted mostly by myself, but later when Buddy Fordham was discharged from the air force, I hunted with him and his friend J.T. Foske, a delightful individual who delivered propane gas. For the first year or so, Spot continued to be an excellent dog. (I've included a cherished photo of him pointing birds at the advanced age of thirteen.) Later, the lion's share of the hunting was done by two dogs: Judge, a lemon-and-white pointer belonging to Buddy, and Belle, a black-and-white drop owned by J.T.

Judge seldom trailed, but excelled at finding both coveys and singles. His only problem was occasional seizures suffered when he became overheated, usually during the early part of the season when temperatures were high. One time we nearly lost him. He had a seizure, fell into a pond, and almost drowned.

The ungainly Belle had a heavily muscled configuration more resembling a bulldog than a bird dog. She ran with a distinctive gait, angling her body to the left, and often seemed about to tip over. At age four Belle had her right hip broken by a tractor, and from then on she had little use of her right hind leg. Still, she remained able to hunt and hunt well. Even with this handicap, Belle could run all day. It was a joy watching her do what she loved. I don't think J.T. ever kept her in a pen. He loaned her to anyone who asked—a recipe guaranteed to ruin a bird dog, but not Belle.

For me, Belle has remained unforgettable. Completely unflappable around untrained dogs, she would remain pointed even when a puppy did his level best to run up birds in front of her. Belle readily shined one day when hunted with a field-trial setter champion from Oklahoma. She put on quite a show. Before the contest, the setter's owner called it "a travesty" that his bred-in-the-purple dog was competing against the humble Belle, but he sang a different tune when the day was over. Belle found ten coveys; the setter found none. Worse, he ran up three of the ones Belle pointed.

Great as Belle was, she couldn't reproduce herself. Bred on several occasions, her offspring proved essentially worthless. In 1963, shortly before I stopped hunting in middle Georgia, J.T. gave Belle to me, and I used her for several years in North Carolina.

Also, I tried a number of other bird dogs and learned how quickly one can fill a dog pen with basically worthless animals. On one occasion our pen held eight pointers who, collectively, couldn't find a crowing barnyard rooster. One pointer we kept was named Spot Junior (after my old dog). He possessed an outstanding nose, and I hunted him for several years. He was the model of a "some-timey" dog. Although sometimes he performed perfectly, he was just as likely to run up covey after covey. No matter what was tried—including some fairly stiff discipline—he didn't change his bad habits.

In 1962, I obtained a liver-and-white pointer, Mack, from a local farmer for the then exorbitant price of one hundred and twenty-five dollars. Two years old and an excellent bird-finder, Mack had been trained by a man who had difficulty walking. Thus, he turned Mack loose to hunt in a field by himself. If Mack didn't return in ten minutes, the owner went looking for him. Such an approach meant Mack had no idea that we were supposed to be partners, and he usually took off in whatever direction that seemed appropriate. To his credit, he was extremely staunch and would stay with a covey all day, if necessary. Mack found a lot of birds, but his self-hunting style resulted in my spending untold hours searching for him.

In middle Georgia, I soon discovered that I knew very little about bird hunting. I had been lulled into thinking of myself as an expert by the abundance of birds in South Georgia. Now to be successful, I had to learn something about finding birds—where and how to hunt.

One positive feature that partially made up for the fewer number of birds was the fact that the singles frequently landed in huntable cover. Interestingly, Spot, a typical "covey dog," didn't share my enthusiasm for single birds. When hunting singles, he would never slow down enough to search the cover adequately, and although he pointed them, he remained ever alert to run off and start hunting for a new covey.

A hunt in middle Georgia typically lasted all day; I'd have stayed longer if the light hadn't given out. The many fences and briar patches that had to be negotiated resulted in torn clothes, gouged skin, and worse. Hunting dawn to dusk allowed me to debunk the widely held belief that quail do not feed until late in the morning. Their activity depends entirely on weather conditions. When the temperature is mild, without a heavy dew or frost, they may feed right after daylight. Also, different coveys on any given day vary markedly in their feeding habits. The frequently espoused notion that all birds in a specific area behave alike is pure nonsense.

Generally, the best time to find quail is from 4:00 P.M. until dark. Often I have had little or no luck, and then, as this witching hour arrived and as if by magic, birds seemed to be everywhere. This fact wasn't lost on our experienced bird dogs, who frequently exhibited little interest in hunting until this magic hour, then suddenly became all business.

Coveys frequently roost in the same general area, and hunting roosting places late in the afternoon often proved productive. Quail scattered by hunters, hawks, or other predators usually begin to whistle recall thirty minutes or so before sundown. Belle learned to listen intently for this whistling, as the birds gathered together, and found quail using both her ears and nose–a remarkable feat, to say the least.

Before I knew better, I flushed roosting birds when it was so dark they were only shapes outlined against a rapidly setting sun. Only much later did I learn that coveys flushed near sundown are especially vulnerable to predators.

Although difficult to imagine in today's more selfish world, farmers back in those days—if asked civilly—frequently allowed bird hunting on their land. I had two experiences while asking permission to hunt that should be inscribed on any list of "Things to Avoid."

J.T.'s father-in-law had a large number of birds on his farm and was quite willing, if forewarned, to let us hunt. On one occasion, while exchanging pleasantries with him before heading out, we made the mistake of letting our dogs run around his yard. I heard a commotion, looked up and saw one of our dogs, either Mack or Judge, tied in a love knot with his small housedog. This act did not endear us at all to the gentleman!

The second situation involved Spot's uncontrollable namesake. Early one morning J.T. and I stopped at a sharecropper's shack to ask permission to hunt. The elderly, bewhiskered, white-haired resident was actively engaged in cooking breakfast, and the pungent odor of frying country ham wafted through the barely-cracked kitchen door as he talked to us.

If we would share our bag of "pottages," he reckoned, the landlord (who lived fifty miles away and wasn't due back for a week) wouldn't mind our hunting.

"Of course we'll share," exclaimed J.T.

"That's fine with me," I said.

But just then, like a flash, Spot Junior dashed between the old man's legs, jumped up on the table, and grabbed the ham. A spate of commotion and cursing followed as Spot sailed out an open window with a half-eaten piece of ham in his mouth. Our welcome disappeared with that ham! After paying for the purloined meat, we hurriedly removed ourselves and our thieving dog from the scene.

Usually I hunted in Bleckley County, but Buddy and I did hunt one day near Albany, on terrain that typified South Georgia—open pine forest with undergrowth of gallberries. We had no way other than "shank's mare" (walking) to cover the ground, and it seemed as if I walked fifty miles that day.

Late in the afternoon we hunted adjacent to one of the "rich Yankee" quail plantations—fenced land with a caretaker constantly on the lookout to drive away poachers. Spot started trailing birds and ventured perhaps fifty yards onto the other side of the fence. I knew he had no business over there, so I grabbed him by the collar, led him back, and turned him loose again.

Undeterred, he quickly returned to the same place, trailed for about seventy-five yards, and pointed. I unloaded my gun, laid it down on my side of the fence, and then ran up the birds he had pointed. *No harm done,* I thought.

Along came the caretaker on his horse. He gave me a vociferous tongue-lashing: "You have no respect for property lines!"

"I'm sorry," I said several times, trying to explain what had happened, but he kept on ranting about how I typified an unprincipled poacher.

Giving up, I left him still raging. Since about half the birds had flown to our side of the fence, I had the supreme pleasure of watching Spot find several singles, which I shot while the caretaker exercised his tongue.

"You should train your birds to stay home," I respectfully opined.

He did not seem grateful for the advice.

We weren't far from the car, and to avoid further confrontation, we left post haste.

I also hunted near Ocilla, Georgia, with a Baptist preacher best described as a "running" type of bird hunter. His behavior made everyone, even the dogs, nervous. Whenever the dogs pointed, he ran to flush the birds, emptying his five-shot, 12-gauge automatic without concern for anyone else's opportunity to shoot. Then, after the display of firepower, he immediately laid claim to all the downed birds.

Although a preacher, he was no gentleman, behaving more like a typical "game hog." We thought about slipping the "Reverend" some shells in which the shot had been removed but decided not to bother. For obvious reasons, I never hunted with him again.

My internship at Duke and military service at the National Heart Institute cut deeply into time I had to spend hunting in middle Georgia. I returned to Durham in 1962, joining the Duke Medical Center faculty as a cardiologist. Within a few years, the majority of middle Georgia bird-hunting venues had been covered with pine forests, which crowded out the quail habitat. Luckily, I found that North Carolina offered a good alternative. By mid-decade, I said "good-bye" to middle Georgia.

The Carolina Years 1962–1987

Chapter IV

Before describing my experiences in North Carolina, I'd like to relate an incident that took place during my "captivity" (living among the Yankees). I must admit, though, it wasn't all bad. While stationed at the National Heart Institute and living in Bethesda, Maryland, Spot kept me company, and together we found a few "Northurn" quail.

Urbanization had occurred at a rapid pace, but there remained some residual farming nearby with reasonably good dove shooting, and even a few areas supporting quail. A most memorable event occurred when I hunted with a colleague, Dr. Chuck Chidsey, who brought along a Weimaraner that had recently been imported from Germany. Chuck, incidentally, built an outstanding medical career in clinical pharmacology, then subsequently found raising horses in Wyoming more to his liking.

Anyway, his Weimaraner, Heidi, the first example of this breed that I had ever seen, viewed the world through a pair of exceptionally "crazy eyes." Had she been a pointer, I would have judged her to be insane. However, Weimaraners were widely touted as excellent, "all-purpose" hunting dogs requiring little, if any, training, so I decided to keep an open mind. If she could do the job, who cared about a demented stare?

Heidi showed no interest whatsoever in what we were doing. She merely walked along with us. Spot found a covey and a few singles, but Heidi remained aloof. Then, without warning, Heidi changed from disinterested stroller to something akin to an excited youngster turned loose in a candy store. She disappeared, bolting into a thick honeysuckle tangle, barked a few times, and reappeared with an enraged and malodorous skunk in her mouth.

Amazingly, the horrible odor didn't trouble Heidi at all, and separating her from this trophy took determination and strength. We felt like fools, wrestling with a dog over a skunk. Luckily, if anything could be called lucky this day, we were only a mile from Chuck's home, and we enticed her into following my car without the necessity of her riding in the trunk.

We washed Heidi in several gallons of tomato juice and tubs of soapy water, which improved the situation, though not to anything really tolerable. I exited as quickly and gracefully as possible, learning later that Heidi was persona non grata in the Chidsey household for several days. For me, the episode ended any curiosity I might have had about the skills of the "all-purpose" Weimaraner breed.

When I moved from Bethesda to Durham, I eagerly sought access to farmland where I could resume serious bird hunting. I didn't have to look far. My maternal grandmother had been raised about twenty-five miles from Durham, on a 260-acre farm in Cedar Grove. This farm adjoined a similar-size tract belonging to a distant cousin. These farms, like many in the Piedmont region of North Carolina, had small-acreage tobacco allotments, and the remainder of the cropland contained corn, wheat, and soybeans, plus about 15 percent in permanent pasture.

Both farms had been more extensively planted in the immediate past; a number of these unused acres had just begun to grow up in weeds, broomstraw, etc. Second-growth pines covered some of the older fields, and most of the woods were mature hardwood with abundant acorns and fairly open, but containing dense tangles of honeysuckle. As far as I know, burning had never been employed to control the underbrush. Still, because winters were more severe than in Georgia, the growth of underbrush had been retarded, and the land remained open for a longer period.

In addition to Cedar Grove, I had access through colleagues and patients to a number of farms in the area. One of the best venues, five-hundred acres of recently clear-cut timberland, became available in 1968, through Mr. Russell Poole of Rougemont, North Carolina. Although Russell hunted birds with me occasionally for ten years, his primary loves were game fowl and fox hunting.

It should be noted that, although at a slower pace than farther South, land taken out of active crop production gradually becomes covered with heavy underbrush and second-growth pines, essentially eliminating the quail habitat. The second factor destructive to quail propagation is urban sprawl. Today, because of almost boomtown growth, much of the area I had previously hunted in Durham and Orange Counties is occupied by housing developments, traffic jams, and shopping centers.

In 1970, I had a unique opportunity and purchased land surrounded by a part of Duke Forest. My twenty-eight acres housed four coveys of birds and provided an opportunity to hunt close to home. I've built a cabin in these woods, and pens to house my bird dogs.

Although this book primarily concerns bird hunting, I want to digress briefly to discuss the fox hunting I did between 1963 and 1966. Mr. John Hardy, a Virginia blueblood by birth, and a dedicated—if somewhat erratic—fox hunter, introduced me to the sport. That first night (we always hunted at night) I went with Mr. Hardy and Big Boy, his dog, who rode like a prince in a one-wheel trailer. When it came time to hunt, Big Boy ambled off about a hundred yards, plopped down, and proceeded to howl all night.

But the night amounted to anything but a bust. I met several dedicated foxhunters, witnessed the skills of several excellent hounds and became fast friends with Mr. Marshall Massey, a former World War II paratrooper who had been awarded both a Silver Star and a Purple Heart.

At this time, 1963, there were essentially no deer in the area, but there was a plethora of red and gray foxes. The standard approach called for turning out three or four "jump" dogs shortly after dark, and once they got a fox up and running, releasing the rest of the dogs. If necessary, we followed the chase from one crossing to the next in a pickup truck. The dogs usually ran within the same five-square-mile area, and the hunt ended just before daylight when the fox decided he'd had enough and re-entered his den. (In this version of night hunting practiced in the South, the fox seldom, if ever, is caught and actually seems to enjoy the chase.) Finally, some portion of the next day had to be spent collecting the dogs. If left alone, however, they eventually would return to the point of release and wait until picked up.

I became quite taken with the sport and acquired a pack of six to eight Walker and July dogs, the two predominant breeds of foxhounds. Weather and work permitting, I hunted at least once a week throughout the year but never became really good at discerning the different voices of the dogs. I had an audiologist check my hearing and learned that, although I could hear reasonably well, my ability to identify different pitches was almost nonexistent.

As indicated, this type of fox hunting leaves little resemblance to the English variety, where the creature primarily at risk is the individual riding a horse "hell-for-leather" cross-country. I once purchased a double indemnity life insurance policy from Lloyds of London, and one exclusion involved death incurred while "riding to hounds." It seems the aristocratic English fox hunters, rather than being the scourge of foxes, are more likely to hurt themselves!

Fox hunters genuinely enjoy and love the music floating from a pack of hounds in full cry. However, not everyone appreciates the symphony. Our hounds occasionally ran near the home of a Duke professor, a wildlife "enthusiast." Early one morning, while waiting for our hounds to trickle back to the release point, the professor drove up in a dilapidated VW beetle, jumped out, and began berating us.

"Your dogs ran too close to my house. They'll disrupt the fish breeding in my pond," he claimed.

I had a hard time not laughing at this utter nonsense, but the more he ranted, the more insulting he became.

"If your dogs persist in crossing my land," he finally said, "I'll be justified in shooting them."

"If my dog gets killed, you'll be next," quipped Marshall.

This conversation ended abruptly—the outraged professor becoming ashen faced and leaving post haste. Luckily, no significant sequelae resulted.

Actually, most of the landowners where we hunted welcomed us. One elderly farmer, Mr. Baldwin, who lived near where we turned out the dogs, went out of his way to say how much he liked hearing their "music."

Mr. Baldwin owned a small house dog whose shrill barking effectively drowned out the music of the pack. It is amazing how one small mutt can make more noise than an entire pack of hounds. One night, with the hounds in great voice, but effectively masked by his dog's wailing, we heard a spate of cursing. A door slammed, and although the dog still barked, the sound was markedly muted.

The next day we learned what had happened. Mr. Baldwin, to quiet the nuisance, had pushed the dog into his outdoor privy and closed the door, whereupon the dog fell through the opening in the seat and became begrimed.

"That's the last straw," the farmer said. "Do you know anyone who might want this dog?"

"I know a lonely little old lady," Marshall slyly intoned. "Make the dog presentable, and I'll take him off your hands."

And he did. What actually happened to the dog? I assumed an "ignorance is bliss" policy. At any rate, we no longer endured his shrill yapping—and enjoyed the music of the pack.

Mr. Baldwin, who farmed with mule-drawn machinery and even refused the use of electricity, voiced a certain down-home perspective on the forces shaping society: "This country started going to hell-in-a-hand-basket when we began eating in the yard and crapping in the house."

Fox hunting reiterated to me the importance of weather on scenting conditions. One night the dogs would run together at top speed without a check; another, they would trail slowly and become widely scattered. Wind (direction and velocity) plus humidity and temperature played major roles in defining the scenting conditions.

In 1966, I found myself in the middle of an exciting chase when suddenly, at a crossing, I discovered the dogs were running a deer. Very soon I realized how difficult the presence of deer makes fox hunting at night. Foxhounds enjoy running deer and it's hard to break them of the habit. Deer generally run over a much wider range than fox and are quite likely to dash across a highway, increasing the possibility that the dogs can be hurt or killed.

I encountered another problem—a growing number of unprincipled hunters who steal foxhounds to use as deer dogs. Indeed, maintaining a good pack of foxhounds in the face of highway deaths and thieves became nearly impossible. Part of my dislike for deer hunting undoubtedly stems from losing a number of stellar foxhounds to either accidents or robbers. Nonetheless, the thrill of listening to a pack of hounds drive a fox on a crisp September or October night remains a fond memory. How I wish I could still hear music from Smokey, Irene, Molly, Frosty, Beulah, and Ray.

The only boring aspect of fox hunting at night is the time spent waiting for the dogs to reappear the next morning. As a general rule, it took until mid-morning before the entire pack was reassembled. In order to pass the time in a somewhat more challenging way than drinking coffee or sleeping, I decided to reinstitute my hobby of butterfly collecting. During my early years, especially while in the Boy Scouts, I collected Lepidoptera, obtaining a reasonably good collection of the butterflies and moths found in north Georgia.

I "dusted off" my butterfly net and the other paraphernalia and began to assemble a collection of the butterfly species indigenous to Piedmont North Carolina. Admittedly, several of my fox-hunting colleagues thought my actions somewhat strange. Certainly, the raising of eyebrows and shaking of heads when I was so engaged was commonplace. On the other hand, undoubtedly I was one of the very few people in North Carolina to have a pickup truck with a gun rack mounted over the rear window (as is usually the case) holding a butterfly net, rather than a shotgun or rifle.

My efforts were rewarded one day when I spied a very unusual specimen. I missed with the net but the ever-resourceful and agile Marshall brought down the quarry in his hat. At any rate, we had collected a very rare natural hybrid (Viceroy/Red-Spotted Purple). I contacted the curator of Lepidoptera at the American Museum of Natural History. My prize is permanently ensconced in that institution, being one of the very few naturally occurring similar hybrids. Nothing else as dramatic happened, but I did manage to while away a number of happy hours expanding my butterfly and moth collection.

To return to my lifelong love, the first thing that struck me regarding North Carolina quail was their size. They are at least 25 percent larger than Georgia quail. Also, they had adapted to life in the open woods by feeding on acorns, pine mast, wild berries, and frequently ranging over a much larger area than their more Southern counterparts. North Carolina birds were usually found in thickets, which made shooting more difficult, especially since I hunted mostly alone. Invariably, a tree or bush was interposed between me and the flushing covey.

In 1963, my second year of serious hunting in the Tarheel State, I sowed six, quarter-acre bird-feed patches at Cedar Grove. The number of birds attracted to these dinner plates astounded me, but local hunters also found the patches, and within a short time the quail were shot out. I decided never again to plant food to attract quail unless I could absolutely control access to the area.

I soon learned that quail were not as plentiful in North Carolina as in either middle or South Georgia, but in an afternoon I could find two coveys, bag four or five birds, and come away from the outing quite satisfied. Many times I returned home empty-handed; a few times I had much better luck. Regardless of the score, I always felt fulfilled.

I don't remember seeing woodcock while hunting in Georgia, but a few times I flushed them in North Carolina, primarily in thick cover around streambeds, while I was looking for single birds. Finding more woodcock coincided with my acquisition of Cricket. Whether she had prior experience with woodcock I do not know, but she excelled at hunting where I didn't want her to hunt—specifically in low-lying swampy areas. Like it or not, Cricket frequently found woodcock.

(I participated for ten years in the annual Woodcock Wing Collection Survey sponsored by the U.S. Fish and Wildlife Service, sending the agency a dozen or so wings per season for inspection.)

When the quail population began decreasing in the 1980s, woodcock became the only available game bird, providing at least a modicum of sport. In my limited experience, they stick (they don't run) extremely well when pointed. After flushing, they fly two to three-hundred yards and are fairly easy to re-locate. Usually found in thick cover, they have a slow, predictable flight pattern that serves them poorly when escaping. In addition, it seems the "wind" from a shotgun is sufficient to bring them down. Most of my bird dogs handle woodcock quite adeptly but refuse to retrieve, presumably due to the thick, fragile feathers that get stuck in their mouths.

I've read many stories extolling the mysterious woodcock as a marvelous game bird. My assessment of this literature is that the stories were written by northerners who never had the opportunity to hunt quail.

For twenty years I hunted almost exclusively in North Carolina, and tried to maintain at least two adequate bird dogs throughout this period. When I moved to Durham, Spot still lived, but he was in his dotage and not effective in the field. Mack and Belle constituted my kennel for several years. I added the aforementioned Cricket, a small liver-and-white pointer who came from a trainer in Kentucky. Extremely energetic and able to cover a lot of ground—a pure joy to watch as she worked a venue—Cricket possessed a mediocre nose but ranked better than average as a bird finder.

In the late 1960s, a patient gave me the year-old granddaughter of Fast Delivery (the equivalent of Secretariat in pointer breeding). This bitch was beautifully made, but became uncontrollable, leaving me to hunt in another county. (I am certain that if electronic collars had been available to control her range, she would have been an outstanding hunting companion.) At any rate, her drive and style impressed me so much that I bred her to an exceptional local bird dog and began training several of the puppies.

Rena, the only one I finally kept, developed into one of my best bird dogs, requiring minimal training, except to make her understand that rabbits were not quail. One time, after I admonished her for paying too much attention to "brer rabbit," she exacted revenge. She pointed at a small honeysuckle thicket, and when I walked in front of her, a large rabbit sped lickety-split from the scene. As I turned to deliver a tongue-lashing, a covey flushed from the same place, startling me so severely I didn't shoot.

Dogs speak with their eyes. Rena shot me a priceless "what-an-idiot-you-are" look. Rena was one of only two pointers I have owned who liked to hunt dead birds and retrieve.

Sandy, my next acquisition, was already well trained and a fine covey dog when I got her. She and Rena complemented each other and became a superb pair. Besides exhibiting a dearth of style, Sandy's only weakness was her deathly fear of cows. She refused even to cross a pasture containing a cow, always insisting on a detour, no matter that it meant running an extra two or three miles.

Gypsy, a liver-and-white female, was another excellent bird dog who, as I say, owned me. Gypsy had the interesting habit of barking when she inadvertently flushed a bird. Although not acceptable in high-class, bird dog circles, this trait I found helpful, particularly when hunting in a dense area. Occasionally, Gypsy treed a squirrel, another off-color habit, but excellent bird finding skills made her eccentricities acceptable. (I also enjoyed an occasional country-fried squirrel.)

I acquired Pepper, my only setter, in 1980 when he was four, from a bootlegger who was soon to be incarcerated. Though Pepper and I had numerous "fallings-outs" regarding his propensity to hunt in directions I didn't want to go, I respected him as an excellent bird finder with a marvelous nose. I hunted him effectively in both North Carolina and Florida.

Tiny, the most energetic dog I ever owned, came to me by a "stroke of good luck." Her owner, a field-trial enthusiast and breeder from High Point, North Carolina, had bred Tiny twice previously, without results. He tried to sell me one of his field trial "flunk-outs," but I found the dog to be a confirmed bolter. The day I took this dog back, Tiny had aborted again. Obviously mad, he blurted out, "Take this bitch." I did, and it was a decision I never regretted. Tiny had average abilities, but I admired her greatly. She made up for her shortcomings with overwhelming desire and hustle.

In the spring of 1986, I purchased Hannah, a seven-month old started puppy, from a trainer in North Carolina, with the stipulation that he complete her training by the next fall. But then he became involved in the outdoor toilet business and had no time to work the dog, which was a first for me, playing second fiddle to a commode. Maybe it was just as well. The approach he had used to teach backing had been so overzealous that Hannah not only would not back, but she absented herself from the environs if she saw another dog pointing.

Feeling that she was close to becoming a blinker, I decided just to let her hunt and not worry about her backing. This proved to be the appropriate plan. Hannah developed into an outstanding, if somewhat opinionated, performer and eventually participated reluctantly in backing duties.

During my bird-hunting career, I've spent a lot of time, effort, and money on many futile attempts to obtain trained bird dogs. In spite of the owner's claim that their "champion" was outstanding, I have witnessed every fault imaginable. Let me describe a few.

By far the worst is the dog that exhibits no interest in hunting and trots around either underfoot or in the opposite direction from where I am hunting, until the brace mate finds quail. This lackluster performer immediately springs into rapid-fire action and invariably runs up the birds. A variation on this theme was exhibited by a Brittany whose sole purpose in life was to chase and attempt to breed. Both male and female dogs were acceptable—it didn't seem to matter. Our relationship culminated violently one day when Belle, while pointing a covey of birds, was accosted by this Lothario.

Another major fault is a dog that hunts and hunts and hunts . . . but never finds quail. The cause is either a very poor nose or a very stupid dog that has yet to understand why he was born.

Dogs that continually get lost are of little use. I'm not describing a hard-going dog that ranges too far and occasionally doesn't return. What I have in mind is a dog that is far too dumb to follow the hunter, preferring to blunder around in the woods, eventually winding up at some local citizen's abode.

Regarding retrieving: I don't insist on a perfect retrieve to hand. However, the dog must be deemed severely faulty if he macerates the quail to a bloody pulp. Even worse is the dog that grabs a downed bird, runs off, and is found burying the remains.

Yes, I've seen it all. The above is only a smattering of the aberrant behavior seen in supposedly "well-trained dogs." Words can't adequately describe my feelings when the owner admits the dog has a fault or two.

The dogs I have kept, although by no means perfect, nonetheless generally excelled as meat dogs. Over the years I did develop my own hunting skills so that I would not be so totally dependent upon a dog—as I had been with Spot in South Georgia, or Judge and Belle in middle Georgia. I started paying close attention to scenting conditions and the types of cover and terrain where quail are likely to be found.

Slipping into a comfortable groove, I did most of my hunting within twenty-five miles of Durham, but seldom hunted all day, even on Saturdays. Hunting from 2:00 or 3:00 P.M., until dark, I indulged my passion at least once or twice a week throughout the season, except on rare occasions when the ground was frozen, covered with snow, or it was raining. I hunted in a number of other locales—southern Virginia, the low country of South Carolina, and eastern North Carolina—but found no better places or more game than close to home.

During the twenty-year period I hunted primarily in Piedmont North Carolina, the dogs and I usually hunted alone, enjoying the solitude. To avoid being labeled as completely antisocial, I occasionally invited a physician colleague from Duke to join me. Generally, these infrequent outings were rated as at least tolerable. On the other hand, I really enjoyed the companionship and hunting with several avid sportsmen. Through a variety of sources, I met several quail hunters and gained access to a number of excellent bird hunting territories. To name a few: O.C. Mitchell (who brought along Sam, an excellent male pointer), Russell Poole and Marshall Massey (mentioned before), Robert Barbee (a full-time coon, part-time bird hunter), and Fred Parker, a longtime friend who currently looks after the bird dogs while I'm playing Great White Hunter in Africa.

In the early 1970s, 100 quail was the legal yearly limit in North Carolina. Usually we didn't keep an accurate tally but killed considerably fewer than that. For some unknown reason one year, Fred kept his tally; he almost made it. But, on the last day, he missed four in a row and had to settle for 98!

Lest I forget, I must recognize Lacy Nichols, a very close friend, who also participated in bird dog feeding chores when I was otherwise involved.

As mentioned, I usually hunted alone, treasuring the solitude and scenery, the escape from the pressure of work, the wonder of the dogs at work and that ultimate thrill—always startling, always unexpected—the sound of the birds when they flush.

After the explosion of activity in deer hunting in the mid-1970s, I briefly went along with the trend but found it, at least for me, seriously lacking as a satisfying sport. The plethora of deer brought an ever-expanding number of nimrods, either staggering through the woods or careening along the roads. Frankly, I feared being in the woods because of the possibility of getting myself or, more importantly, a good bird dog, whacked by an overzealous or inebriated deer hunter.

Deer season ends January first. Since most of the best weather conditions for bird hunting in North Carolina end before the first of the year, my reluctance to risk being killed surely contributed to the decreasing number of quail I found during the late 1970s and early 1980s. Another drawback involved the amount of land I had available for hunting, which was gradually dwindling due to urban sprawl and the inevitable growing-up of unused farmland into dense pine thickets. Then, when it appeared that things couldn't get worse, they did.

Between 1984 and 1986, the few remaining birds essentially disappeared, and although I have hunted occasionally since then, I've found a total of less than five coveys. Formerly, I frequently found that many in a single day.

In the 1980s, I tried preserve hunting in Asheboro and Mebane, North Carolina. The quail had been released just before I arrived and offered little of the challenge their wild brethren presented. I also joined a hunting club near the Eastern Shore, which promised wild bird hunting, but it soon became apparent that the claims were false: The quail had been freshly released.

Describing my upland bird hunting experiences in North Carolina would be incomplete without mentioning the mourning dove. Dove hunting on a fairly grand scale is a common North Carolina phenomenon and frequently assumes a festive atmosphere around Labor Day. The hunting ranges from a small group of hunters covering a field of freshly cut silage, to an enormous gathering of shooters who come together not only to hunt, but for a social gathering and "pig-pickin" (a whole pig is roasted over hickory coals, and guests make pigs of themselves).

For my money, when rating upland birds for difficulty in wingshooting, doves rank at the top of the list. You must be a good shot to bring them down consistently. Why, then, don't I enjoy dove hunting? There are three reasons: 1) Pointers aren't involved, though I've seen a few hearty souls try to use them to retrieve doves—a major waste of talent, in my estimation; 2) I do not like crowds; and 3) September is too hot in North Carolina. When the late part of the dove season arrives, it usually coincides with the quail season, and there is no question as to my choice. I have to admit, however, that I have been on some impressive dove hunts, if numbers seen and killed are any yardstick.

I am convinced that when dove hunting, I have an unerring propensity for taking a position in that part of the field where the doves are not flying. An additional example of my poor judgment: I always find the slowest moving supermarket checkout lane (all the others zip along smoothly while mine runs out of billing tape, needs a price check, or requires the presence of a hard-to-find manager to resolve some earth-shattering dispute). Try as I might to calculate the best location scientifically by tracking the doves' flight patterns, I nonetheless always seem to watch them fly over someone else. Therefore, if I do shoot at all, I am shooting at them second or third, which makes for a more sporty, but less successful, outing.

I confess I have learned no particular tricks about dove shooting, except to pick a stand in the open, so that after they fall they can be easily found. If the birds go down in thick cover, the majority of the hunt will be spent tramping around trying to find them.

Immediately after killing a bird, I retrieve it, because waiting and continuing to shoot results in my being unable to locate it later. Since killing the legal limit usually is readily accomplished, missing the chance to shoot while retrieving is not a major problem.

Although doves are tough birds and can keep flying after being wounded, they are not immortal. Like other hunters unable to admit shortcomings as shooters, however, I have found myself claiming that many doves continued to fly after I'd "shot their hearts out."

The key to shooting doves is to fire at them only when they're within a reasonable range—not more than thirty-five yards. Most doves are missed or, worse, wounded by trigger-happy dimwits who fire when the birds are far out of range. This unsportsmanlike behavior is reinforced when a dove fifty yards off occasionally falls. Shotgun shell manufacturers may be delighted by these Annie Oakley wannabes, but the result is needlessly wounding doves.

Granted, it may be difficult judging distances in a dove field, but, prior to shooting, stepping off the distance to a few markers can solve the problem. Doves do fly fast; it's hard to lead them too much. Often when firing at the lead bird in a flock, I have hit one several yards behind the leader.

Throughout the twenty-plus years I've hunted in North Carolina, a variety of memorable events occurred. But the incidents etched most clearly in my memory all involve quail hunting. A few of the most notable vignettes follow.

I shall never forget one evening at dark when I missed Pepper. I finally found him, after searching for an hour by flashlight, beside a honeysuckle thicket where he lay on his right side, no longer able to stand but still on a rigid point—the covey roosting in a tight circle a few feet away.

Once, by pure luck, I hit a quail in the head with one pellet that caused a straight-up flight, almost out of sight. This event was observed by Tiny, who caught the bird in her mouth as it plummeted earthward, much like a Frisbee.

After a covey flushed from a honeysuckle thicket and flew in a bunch through the only available opening, I killed six quail with one shot—the pellets arriving at the same time the birds did.

One bitterly cold, dark day Rena jumped into a pond covered by ice to retrieve a quail. She broke through the ice but managed to grab the bird and somehow got back to shore. I nearly cried when, bedraggled and cold, she presented her prize to me.

I spied Gypsy pointing under a small pine tree. As I approached within fifty yards or so, a large raccoon sailed out of the pine, flushed the birds, and scampered up a nearby oak, disappearing into a convenient hole. The quail left our part of the world unhurt, and Gypsy and I could do nothing but curse the meddling coon.

In fields overgrown by young pine trees, a flushed covey may escape unseen and unhurt—but not always. Pepper pointed in the middle of such a thicket, and as I walked toward him, it became obvious that there was only one narrow opening for the birds to fly where I could shoot—very unlikely odds.

As I stepped in front of him, a bird flushed and flew just right—an easy shot. Pepper didn't move. One more step, and another bird took the same route. Pepper didn't move. This scenario was repeated six more times. Finally, Pepper broke and retrieved the two birds. (I could have wiped out the entire covey, but I didn't shoot at the last six.) Why the birds behaved in such an agreeable way, or how Pepper could count to eight, is still a mystery.

One unforgettable afternoon, Mack and Belle pointed at the edge of a soybean field. When I arrived, the birds had moved off, and the dogs began trailing through an old pasture sparsely covered with broomstraw. I spotted the covey about seventy yards off, hustling toward a honeysuckle tangle at the edge of the pasture. I'd had little prior experience with moving quail and considered running toward the covey in order to force them to flush. Just then Belle stopped trailing. She made a wide detour, placed herself between the covey and the thicket, and pointed. The birds were trapped! I approached the huddled bevy in a leisurely fashion and downed a double.

Never before or since have I seen a similar occurrence. I have heard tales, and assumed they were lies, about dogs that could herd birds, but I never expected to see such a thing. Whether Belle thought out her actions, I shall never know, but I still remember and treasure every aspect of her performance.

Yes, twenty-plus years of indelible memories, and I am forever grateful.

The Florida Years 1980 and Beyond

Chapter V

Beginning

The first time I hunted quail in Florida was 1975, as a guest of Dr. Jack Flanagan, a longtime friend. (I met Jack when we were medical residents at Duke Medical Center.) We hunted near Immokalee on a ranch owned by one of Jack's patients.

The trip to Immokalee marked another first—hunting from a vehicle, in this case, a Jeep. I didn't take my dogs; we hunted with several wide-ranging pointers belonging to a friend of our host. In terms of number of birds found, the trip proved very successful. We found eight to ten coveys per day. I noted the quail were smaller and the males darker in color than those found farther north. In addition, both coveys and singles tended to run, rather than freeze, when pointed. I genuinely enjoyed this trip and hoped subsequent forays would be forthcoming, but it took five years before the invitation came again, and not a moment too soon, because by 1980, the quail-hunting opportunities in North Carolina were fast disappearing.

Jack had arranged for two venues in central Florida: A cattle ranch near Wauchula and a hunting preserve belonging to the International Minerals Corporation (IMC) close to Myakka City. We hunted one day at the former, three at the latter. The flat terrain in these areas contained scattered pine trees and the ground was covered with wiregrass, gallberries, and low bush palmettos, with about 10 percent in improved pasture. Yearly burning and cattle grazing kept the underbrush controlled. Feeders, either a plastic or metal drum containing cracked corn and protected by a cattle and hog-proof fence, were used to attract quail.

We hunted coveys from a Jeep or pickup truck equipped with a dog box and a seat above the box for the hunters. It concerned me initially that the dogs, accustomed to my being on the ground with them, would have difficulty with this new approach, but they adapted quickly. Nor have I had problems subsequently with dogs that were trained for foot hunting becoming accustomed to my loafing on a vehicle rather than walking. An obvious advantage is the fact that the pointers spend most of the time looking for quail instead of me.

Due to the inevitably hot and dry weather, scenting conditions in our Florida venues were tenuous. The best hunting occurred in the morning, 8:00 to 10:30 A.M., shortly after the dew evaporated, plus the hour before sundown. With rare exceptions, the dogs could not locate birds during the rest of the day, and because of the heat they became quickly exhausted if hunted during this time.

Ralph, the IMC majordomo responsible for maintaining the preserve, stocked his kennel with a plethora of mediocre bird dogs. Of necessity, we relied primarily on mine. That first year, to avoid a twelve-hour drive, Rena and I flew to Tampa. Rena was in her prime and a superb bird dog, but on the return flight the airline didn't transfer her at Atlanta, and she went on to Chicago. There, exposed to subzero temperatures, she caught pneumonia and was nearly dead when she finally arrived back in Durham. I am still angry—and always will be—at that now-defunct airline. As a consequence, I began to drive the long journey to Florida, carrying Pepper, Gypsy, and, later, Tiny. In addition, Jack brought along a reasonably good pointer bitch.

The IMC dogs had learned the "feeder trick." Rather than hunt, they ran from one feeder to the next, pointing whether or not quail were present. This problem soured me on the use of surface feeders. My dogs had no experience with them, but it didn't take them very long to pick up the bad habit.

Another difficulty arose when the quail near the feeders heard the approaching vehicle and ran to the nearest impenetrable thicket. To outsmart the birds (though sometimes it didn't work), we began parking several hundred yards away and walking to the feeder.

Pepper and Gypsy adapted reasonably well to the differences in hunting conditions between Florida and North Carolina, and paid little attention to strange new critters: a wide variety of water birds, snipe, armadillos, and feral hogs. Still, to repeat, our chief difficulty involved poor scenting conditions. Pepper consistently outperformed the other dogs and made me appreciate the importance of a good nose. Thanks mainly to him, we averaged finding six coveys a day.

Unfortunately, after three years, a change in tax laws persuaded IMC to drop its quail-management program. We continued to have permission to hunt, but the undergrowth became such that within two years the quail were gone. Also, truck farming occupied a significant part of the land. What had been a favorite venue became a thousand-acre tomato field.

In 1984, I met Mr. Roy Vandegrift, a very successful sweet-corn truck farmer. Roy invited me to hunt on his ranch at Yee Haw Junction, Florida, a four thousand acre spread. Roy didn't hunt, but he did enjoy watching turkey and deer and had developed the ranch to provide an optimal habitat for these species. He planted approximately five hundred acres in fairly large fields with various types of grain and supplemented the larder with a daily distribution of cracked corn. Roy had launched his program just two years before I arrived on the scene, and the number of turkey and deer already present can best be described as amazing. From a blind near one of the feeding stations, I have counted as many as two hundred turkeys and fifty deer at one time. No one was allowed to hunt them, but Roy accorded me the privilege of being the lone quail hunter.

There were no cattle on the ranch. Roy had tried burning, but part of a cypress swamp became too hot and thus damaged a number of trees he wanted to conserve. Ruling out further burning, he spent countless hours at great expense disking and chopping fields, but the vegetation on the rest of the land rapidly became too dense to survive. A vivid illustration of this problem occurred on a three hundred acre field. This land was planted in pine trees in order that the ranch could be designated a tree farm. Initially, this area housed seven or eight coveys, but within two years the undergrowth became so thick that the birds disappeared.

For the first year or two, I coordinated my trip to Roy's ranch with hunting at the IMC spread. At Roy's, I used Tiny, Pepper, and, later on, Hannah, and rode on a seat affixed to the dog box in the back of my truck, but I covered the birdy areas on foot. On average, I found six or seven coveys a day, plus some pretty good single bird shooting.

For three to four years the hunting was ideal. But then, Roy sold half the property, which contained some of the best hunting land, and the undergrowth on the rest proliferated to the point that only a few hundred acres of good quail habitat remained.

Enter Joey O'Bannon

In 1985, I hunted on the ranch near Immokalee, where ten years earlier I had been introduced to quail hunting in Florida. The intervening years had not been kind to the local quail population, and my sojourn proved largely unfruitful. My host, however, mentioned that his nephew had opened a quail hunting preserve under the rubric of J&R Outfitters, west of LaBelle.

"Why not check it out?" he suggested. I'm glad I did.

This preserve, located on sixteen thousand acres of sparse pine forest, had an undergrowth of wiregrass, low bush palmettos, and contained a number of boggy slews. A few thousand acres were used for truck farming, while the remainder fed grazing cattle. The quail preserve occupied about a thousand acres.

The quail, which were fed milo and cracked corn, were released in coveys of ten to twelve birds. Every effort was made to simulate wild bird hunting. Managing the operation was Joey O'Bannon, who had learned the nuances of guiding and tending to quail from his grandfather, who had performed those duties on the magnificent Phipps plantation.

Joey, a dedicated cowboy, took awhile before entering the guiding business. He decided, after his thirtieth birthday and several serious mishaps, that his future resided somewhere other than in rodeo. He knew about quail and hunting, and, thus, he became a professional guide. From our first meeting, Joey and I began to develop what has become a warm and lasting friendship.

Various Venues

My prior experiences (in North Carolina) with released birds had been unsatisfactory, but in Florida the difference between released and wild bird hunting was not as obvious. The first afternoon, Joey and I found a large covey of native quail. It occurred to me that I might make a deal with him to allow me to hunt the wild birds on the sixteen thousand acres of ranchland to which he controlled the hunting rights. Indeed, in 1986, we did strike this bargain. I have hunted almost exclusively with Joey since then, averaging six trips per year, four or five days each trip.

In the beginning, I drove nonstop to the hunting venues, using the twelve hours to enjoy conservative talk radio and audio-tapes, ranging from Shakespeare to Hank Williams. More recently, I have given up this arduous drive and instead fly to West Palm Beach, where I arrive refreshed and ready to hunt.

I hunted on the ranch at LaBelle until 1989, when J&R Outfitters moved to a four thousand acre tract near Indiantown, Florida. A former sod farm, this new ranch had considerable acreage in improved pasture and boggy areas, much of which was overgrown with myrtle. Whereas at LaBelle we averaged six coveys per day, the count near Indiantown dropped to three. Also, the thick cover of myrtle made shooting more difficult. To assure a sufficient number of birds to hunt, I began relying on acclimated quail that had been released a month or so earlier.

In 1993, I leased twenty-seven hundred acres of excellent quail habitat near Hobe Sound, Florida, that had not been managed for a number of years. My experiences at the IMC preserve and Yee Haw Junction demonstrated that a major hindrance to quail propagation in Florida is the rapid growth of underbrush; it becomes so thick "you can't hit the ground with a tomahawk," and then the quail disappear. This was the case at Hobe Sound.

The best method to control undergrowth is frequent burning, usually on an every-other-year rotation. Contrary to what one might guess, the burns attract quail. I have watched them feed on still-smoking, freshly burned ground. Although controlled burning is reasonably safe, it is an impressive and frightening sight: A wall of fire fifteen feet high, igniting two hundred acres in twenty to thirty minutes. However, there are two minor negatives about burning. The stubble makes the dogs sore footed, and clothing quickly becomes filthy. Moreover, near the lease in Hobe Sound are several "high-end" condominiums, and the occupants do not seem to appreciate the positive aspects of controlled burning. Invariably, they create a ruckus.

Livestock also plays an essential role in reducing underbrush. I actually grew fond of Florida cattle. These part-Brahma cows don't seem to be "hell-bent" on attacking my dogs and me, as did their woods cousins in South Georgia.

I had high hopes for the Hobe Sound acreage. In addition to burning, Joey expended an enormous amount of effort in chopping the area to make it suitable for quail. The birds responded, and after three years the number of coveys increased significantly. However, a tropical storm left twenty-four inches of water behind, immersing the entire area except for a few high canal banks. It took several weeks for the water to recede and the bird population was, to say the least, decimated. We tried to be philosophical, but after two more years and a nearly total absence of quail, I gave up. In addition, the owner decided that the cost of the annual lease should triple. Good-bye Hobe Sound.

In searching around for additional venues, we hunted for several years on a large ranch, used primarily for deer hunting, near Bassinger, about fifty miles from Indiantown. Quail were never particularly numerous, but on occasion, we did find four to six coveys a day.

Luckily, the situation in Indiantown markedly improved. Joey was able to obtain permanent control of the acreage. He carried out extensive burning and chopping, and he opened the canals to facilitate drainage. These efforts markedly improved the habitat for quail. In addition, he decided to stock the area with water buffalo and a variety of other exotic game. This required construction of an eight-foot game fence around the entire ranch. Significant predation of some of the small deer by coyotes became a serious problem. He instituted a series of strategies to get rid of the coyotes and a very impressive number were killed.

I had no idea how destructive coyotes were, but lo and behold, within two years, the quail population dramatically increased. In fact, wild coveys of twenty to thirty birds were essentially everywhere. Thus, I concentrated my hunting efforts on this ranch. The only drawback, again, has been the result of several recent hurricanes inundating the area with water and drowning a number of the young quail. This seems to be a constant problem in this section of Florida, but I have learned to "live with it." At any rate, at least for the present, we have a very stable and excellent population of quail. In fact, recently I found myself becoming impatient if we go as long as thirty minutes without finding birds. Frankly, I'm "spoiled rotten."

Pointers That Point . . . Usually

On my first trip to LaBelle, I hunted with Pepper, Tiny, and Bubba, a four-year-old meat dog that belonged to Joey. Bubba did not have a particularly good nose but did possess a high degree of bird sense. His only fault was that if he spied quail on the ground, he was seized by an uncontrollable urge to force them airborne. While not a particular detriment when hunting released birds, it posed a serious problem when hunting native quail running out of shotgun range.

When I decided to hunt almost exclusively near LaBelle, the acquisition of several topflight bird dogs became mandatory, a quest that continues to this day. Previously, my bird-hunting adventures had been successfully carried out with two or three good dogs, but at LaBelle, because of the heat and amount of territory to be covered, I needed a minimum of six. There are many winter days with adequate cloud cover when the maximum temperature is sixty degrees, making it possible to hunt the majority of daylight hours. Staying at it four and five days in a row, therefore, requires a well-stocked kennel.

There is also another significant problem: If the dogs are not hunted frequently, they cannot perform at top level. Thus, Joey and I reached an agreement: He would use my dogs to hunt in the preserve with selected clients.

After two years of hunting in LaBelle, any opportunities to find quail in North Carolina became virtually nonexistent. Thus, I left Hannah with Joey, who instantly developed a love/hate relationship with her. He loved her ability and willingness to work but hated her surly attitude.

Hannah had more bottom than any bird dog I ever owned. She would hunt with one dog until he had to rest, then continued with another until he could go no further, and finally, she would wear out still another. For four or five years, Hannah and Bubba were Joey's primary dogs. His many clients bagged an average of ten-to-fifteen-thousand birds per year over their points.

Hannah and Bubba were fairly wide-ranging but hunted a pattern to the front. Locator beeper collars weren't available at the time, so I spent many hours searching for them and guessing their whereabouts, primarily using the "force" to find them—invariably pointed.

Pepper began to backslide and, at LaBelle, was only marginally effective. After the second year, a year of constantly being outdone by his brace mates, his behavior deteriorated even further. Running behind most of the time, he began killing armadillos and baby pigs. (It's depressing—saddening, really—when either old dogs or old men cannot accept the results of aging and resort to childish behavior.)

I continued to carry Tiny back and forth with me, but the other dogs, like rich "snowbird" Yankees, wintered in Florida and summered up north. Tiny continued, by far, as my best retriever.

I purchased a three-year-old, well-trained female named Lib from a man in Asheboro, North Carolina, with the stipulation that he could raise a litter of her puppies. Lib developed into a dog any hunter would be proud of, despite having an obnoxious drawback. Any quail she retrieved got bisected by a through-and-through bite. For my part of Lib's puppy deal, I ended up with Bonnie, who became a competent, but not brilliant-like-her-mother, bird dog.

Anne, a two-year-old, partially trained dog from Lib's previous litter, came up for sale at a bargain-basement price. In a hurry, I put her in the truck without examining her closely. Only when I arrived at home did I learn the reason for the low cost. She was undoubtedly the most poorly configured dog I had ever owned. You name the fault; she had it—a real ugly duckling. Worse, she was allergic to fleas and had a serious skin rash that required steroid treatment. No matter. I fell in love with Anne. She was a delight in the pen, always good-natured and full of life and fun.

"What is that?" Joey asked, when I arrived in LaBelle with Anne.

"A bird dog," I replied. "A good one."

"This is some kind of joke, right?"

"Wait till you see her in action."

"She looks to be about two-thirds foxhound," Joey muttered, as he shrugged his shoulders and scanned the heavens for help.

But not every good pointer must look as if bred-in-the-purple. Joey, a practical man, soon became enamored of Anne as well. She performed superbly in the field, learning to handle both released and wild birds with ease. She had more desire to hunt than even Hannah, more than any dog I have ever owned.

A rattlesnake bit Lib the second year I hunted her (the only dog I've owned that was bitten while hunting). Right away I injected intravenously two vials of antivenom, and although the left leg swelled considerably, she survived. Remarkably, after a two-week rest, she returned to hunting. I had her spayed at the end of the season and was stunned when she died during the procedure by a cause unknown.

After Lib died, I projected a major shortage of dogs for the coming year and succumbed to a severe panic attack that resulted in the loss of my reasoning powers. The bottom line was that I bought three pointers from a field-trial trainer. The first turned out to be totally useless, but the second, a two-year-old half brother to a national champion, was tough as iron and made an excellent bird dog. His name was Hank. In order to force released quail to fly out of gallberry and myrtle thickets, Joey let him flush. The result was that Hank became too aggressive and could not be trusted on wild quail.

By far the most expensive acquisition was Flirt, a stylish three year old that had been campaigned extensively in shoot-to-retrieve trials where, though robotic in manner, she achieved considerable success. I had the mistaken notion that performing well in these trials would equate to excellence in bird hunting. Not so, at least in the case of Flirt, undoubtedly the most thickheaded bird dog I have ever owned. She never learned even to follow the truck and had no inkling where to search for quail.

In 1988, I obtained Lib's other daughter, Lib II, an untrained, but extraordinarily active dog. She exceeded all expectations at age two but never progressed further in developing bird sense. In fact, Lib II would just as soon hunt in a shallow pond as in birdy areas. Accordingly, she didn't find many birds, but handled what she did locate in a most professional manner. If allowed to run excessively, Lib II suffered seizures, probably from hypoglycemia.

I bred Hank to Lib II, and from the litter of four puppies I kept and trained two. The other two were killed, one by a rattlesnake and the other from rat poison. One of the puppies that made it, Luke, became in all regards a standout bird dog. He developed a stress fracture of his right foreleg, which never healed properly; he became lame if hunted more frequently than every third day.

Faith, the other puppy, had the best nose of any bird dog I have ever hunted. It amazed me to watch her as a puppy, running from bird to bird, as if pulled by her nose. In her second year, she exhibited a bad case of the "terrible twos," trying every way possible to be obnoxious—unusually obnoxious. She was, however, a real "brag dog." Her ability to work effectively in poor scenting conditions bordered on the miraculous.

In the mid 90s, after much trial and error, I obtained five first-rate bird dogs—Poppy, Sugar, Fanny, Missy, and Cody—from a trainer in Texas named Jarrett Thompson. It took several months for these dogs to adjust to hunting in Florida, but each of them was a pleasure in the field. Missy and Cody produced eight puppies, named after Shakespearean characters. Seven of them—Kate, Portia, Miranda, Prince Hal, Horatio, Hamlet, Humphrey—became acceptable bird dogs. Horatio, Hamlet, and Humphrey were really outstanding in every way. Hamlet was killed by a trigger-happy client. This unfortunate event caused Joey to temporarily curtail using my dogs to hunt with clients. Out of necessity, he acquired five or six additional dogs. Frankly, only one of them, Lou, a double cross of Missy, turned out to be a high-class bird dog.

Through a misunderstanding of her breeding, Lou was bred to her uncle. After expending considerable time and effort, essentially only one dog from this inbred litter, Luke (The Younger), turned out to be a keeper. Except for periodically forgetting to straighten out his tail while on point, he is a real bird-finding machine. Luke reverses the adage that a "pointer is far more stylish when pointing than pissing."

In 2001, I obtained a very stylish lemon-and-white male pointer, Jeb, from Jarrett Thompson. Jeb was an outstanding dog. An additional benefit is that now we don't have a kennel completely filled with black-and-white pointers. Jeb's only drawback: Being tender-mouthed was not part of his makeup, very much like Tiny. In fact, he never brought in a wounded bird. Usually, the retrieved quail appeared to have been "tenderized" with a mallet. Unfortunately, Jeb lost his left eye in an altercation with a palmetto bush, but he continued to be a star performer. (This includes being a "ladies' man" and papa on several occasions.)

Jeb and Lou produced three puppies, Scylla, Charybdis, and Ulysses. For some inexplicable reason at age nine months they exhibited all the style, bird-finding abilities, and class of a four-year-old brag dog. These puppies were so impressive at an early age that we bred Lou to Jeb the next time she came in heat. She gave birth to two puppies, but decided that the chores of motherhood were no longer acceptable. She refused to have anything to do with her progeny. Tyre and Troy were bottle-fed and thrived.

Of the three older dogs, Ulysses and Scylla continued to develop into stylish bird-finding machines. Charybdis, possessing the best nose, developed an unfortunate characteristic requiring culling. (I had seen this problem once before with Portia.) In the presence of nearby quail, he slows down and walks in a semipointed fashion until he locates the birds. This fault was not the result of being punished excessively for running up birds, i.e., Charybdis was not over-broke. I thought that, with time and experience, the problem would disappear. It got worse. To make a long story short, now he resides in Colorado and is reported to be a top-notch pheasant dog.

Tyre and Troy were quite different: Troy exhibited enumerable culling characteristics. On the other hand, Tyre hunted hard, found quail, pointed, but showed no excitement with the proceedings. About one year of age, while hunting in a thick slew, he found a scattered covey of birds. His behavior changed dramatically; it was as though a light went on in his head. He pointed, retrieved the downed bird, and then proceeded to point seven or eight more birds sequentially. From that moment on, he was "bird crazy" and rapidly developed into a top-notch covey dog. Although a rare characteristic in a big-going pointer, Tyre is also an accomplished single-bird dog. In fact, his ability to locate rapidly all the single birds in a scattered covey is nothing short of miraculous. Coupled with his two older siblings, Scylla and Ulysses, they constitute an outstanding threesome.

Jeb was bred to Diana, a daughter of Hamlet, whose only fault was slight ticking while on point. Virgo, the only "keeper" from this litter, was headstrong to the extreme. She required a lot of "personal attention," but a very superior nose made the annoyance worthwhile. Like her namesake, Virgo is a celestial standout.

In the fall of 2006, Joey went to the pen to get Jeb for the day's activities. Jeb was dead. Although only nine years old, he showed no evidence of slowing down; the cause of his death is an unfortunate mystery. Luckily, he left a great legacy in his progeny.

Shortly thereafter, I contacted Mr. Thompson and obtained a two-and-one-half-year-old, lemon-and-white male, Bard. He is a "class act." Except for a propensity to climb out of the kennel, he has no major faults. I was so delighted with him that I bred him to Scylla. Pepper, a four-year-old, liver-and-white female, also emigrated from Texas in 2007 and immediately became a member of the "first team."

After the dogs made their annual pilgrimage to Durham in 2007, Scylla became the proud mother of ten puppies: seven females and three males. One puppy was so small that I took on the added chore of bottle-feeding. "Runtsky" (formally christened Arcturus) survived and caught up with his siblings. Scylla raised the rest—a very impressive litter of puppies. I named them for first magnitude stars. Unfortunately, when six months old, only Rigel and Deneb demonstrated adequate promise to undergo further training, proving once again that breeding "the best to the best" is no guarantee of uniform success.

Pursuing Quail

A major bird-hunting innovation, the electronic shock collar, became available, at least to me, in 1990. This device more or less has eliminated the problem of dogs hunting out of control and "trashing." An even more useful device, the beeper locator collar, also came on the scene. No longer did I have to worry about whether a dog out of sight was pointing or running aimlessly. When I reflect on the countless hours spent searching for dogs, I appreciate what a boon this invention is. Interestingly, although the sound from the beeper collar doesn't seem to disturb quail (a major plus), it appears to jump every deer within hearing distance.

Unfortunately, a significant drawback in using the beeper collar has resulted recently from my unilateral hearing loss. For those of you who are not aware of this problem, if only one ear works, the sounds are easily perceived, but there is no way to designate the direction of the origin. Thus, I can hear the beep, but I can't tell where the dog is pointing. Joey is of little help since his hearing has deteriorated to the point that he doesn't even hear the signal.

So here we are—the dog on point but not visible. I can hear the beep, but the origin is obscure. Even trying to turn around to determine which direction is the loudest, I usually misjudge by a considerable arc. The only thing that really does work is to start walking in one direction until the beep is no longer audible—that's the wrong direction. Then I turn around and go back and start all over again. Obviously, this approach takes considerable time. Frequently, by the time we find the dog, the birds have fled the scene. In the long run, it's still better than returning to the prior approach of using the "force" to find the pointing dog.

The combination of shock collar and beeper collar around the neck adds nothing to the aesthetic stature of the pointing dog, but I accept this minus because of the utility of these devices.

Three years ago, Joey developed an important innovation to the shooting of released birds: He began to use Labradors and, more recently, cocker spaniels (imported from England) to flush and retrieve the birds. The pointers remain pointed while the covey is flushed. In classic quail hunting, the hunter flushes the birds, but many times released birds aren't impressed (scared?) by the human and refuse to fly. Also, native quail have a tendency to run in palmetto thickets and remain on the ground. But a good flushing dog can quickly gain their attention and force them airborne. Using a flush dog keeps the pointers from developing the bad habit of crowding released birds, a fault that renders them unreliable on native quail.

I had witnessed Labradors retrieving quail on a "high society" quail plantation several years before in South Georgia, and felt that it distracted from the hunting experience. However, the reality of released birds makes the situation quite different. We had virtually ruined several dogs, e.g., Hank, for hunting wild birds by letting them run up released birds. Joey's innovation allows our bird dogs to be effective in either situation.

I hunted from a pickup truck during my first few years in Florida, but switched readily, about ten years ago, to a swamp buggy (a platform built on a frame featuring large tractor tires and made to be driven from the top). Swamp buggies are constructed from worn-out trucks and are subjected to frequent submersion in mud and water. They give the impression that they're always falling apart, yet they are remarkably serviceable; mechanical problems frequently seem to "heal themselves." Recently, Joey designed and built a "custom" buggy for us. There were enough cages for ten dogs and weatherproof boxes for the guns. It is an ideal vehicle with one exception: The rear axle cracked three times. Oh well! Nothing is perfect. In fact, after solving this problem, the buggy has been very serviceable.

The advantages of this mode of transportation are threefold: Joey and I can sit together and solve the world's problems while hunting; we are not constrained by terrain, except extremely deep ponds; and our elevated perch lets us see the dogs most of the time.

When compared to hunting in North Carolina, quail were easier for me to kill during my early years of Florida hunting, primarily because of the more open terrain. My skills as a gunnerman gradually deteriorated, and so I looked for ways to slow the inexorable march of time.

I had been shooting a seven-and-a-half pound, 12-gauge Parker, but after reading articles indicating that a lighter gun would improve my score on quail, I revisited the past and began using my grandfather's 20-gauge Parker. It didn't improve my shooting. Later, about fifteen years ago, I obtained a 12-gauge Purdey, weighing six pounds, four ounces, and grew very fond of this gun. I found it easy to switch from the heavy, single-trigger Parker to the lighter much-better-balanced, double-trigger Purdey. My shooting improved considerably for a time but recently has slipped again.

I think I've done everything possible to become a better shot, at least where the hardware is concerned. As for my part, a weekly regimen of shooting skeet would likely help, but since I am basically lazy and really don't give a damn if I miss a few birds (even more than a few), frequent skeet-shooting probably doesn't lie in my future.

An interesting aspect of my "ups and downs" as a marksman has become obvious in the last two to three years. When I arrive at the ranch, I shoot reasonably well for the first day or so. Then things seem to go to "hell in a hand basket" and improve to acceptable levels only on the last day. Joey figured out the problem.

"Doc, you ain't young. Huntin' all day and carousing all night is a thing of the past. You get too tired to use a shotgun properly."

He's right. So what can I do about it? Rest more and hunt only one half day? No way! I had rather watch the bird dogs run and point. I'll continue the "all-day" program, while cussing at my poor performance.

Hunting "Lesser" Fowl

In 1989 I learned about sage grouse in Wyoming, a new (for me) type of bird hunting. The prior year, Joey had experimented briefly with our pointers hunting sage grouse and gave me a favorable report. Although dubious, I went—and thoroughly enjoyed the experience. For ten years, Joey and I hunted for three to four days each September near Farson, Wyoming, a town of 325 hardy souls, between Jackson Hole and Rock Springs. He drove the dogs to Wyoming, and I followed by plane.

It didn't take too long to learn that sage grouse are frequently found in coveys and tend to flush easily. Several of our dogs learned to handle them quite well. Since we hunted grouse in wide-open spaces (you don't get much more wide open than the Wyoming sage country), the chance to watch a bird dog running intricate, precise patterns a half mile or so from the truck has given me stunning, priceless mind pictures that I'll carry always.

In 2002, the season for sage grouse was reduced to only one week long in late September. For the ensuing two years, I was caught in a blizzard and could not hunt, spending the time in Sitzmann's Motel. Although not being particularly bright, I did take the hint, and we gave up sage grouse hunting.

Another interesting diversion from quail has been hunting pheasant in Florida. Three to four times a year, J&R Outfitters sponsors what is called a "tower shoot," in which several hundred pheasants are released from a high platform. The pheasants fly over twelve shooters and, depending on weather conditions and marksmanship, between fifty and one hundred of them land unscathed and escape into the countryside. Freedom, however, is short-lived; the pheasants generally last only about a month before getting killed by hunters or varmints.

I try to arrive a few days after one of these extravaganzas. The surviving pheasants provide a different experience for the dogs. In Florida, released pheasants, like their wild brethren, frequently run. Even when scenting conditions are poor, the dogs have little difficulty trailing, probably because the birds release considerable scent.

My only previous pheasant hunting occurred in the 1980s when a colleague, Dr. Bob Bauman, invited me to hunt near What Cheer, Iowa, some fifty miles southwest of Des Moines. The territory consisted of rolling cropland (the soybeans and corn had been harvested). A significant portion of unplanted acreage had been placed in the Conservation Resource Program, which paid the owner to maintain the land in its natural state.

I hunted pheasants near What Cheer for three successive years, two to three days each time. Bob and I flew to Des Moines, rented a van, and used his dogs—a pointer, a Brittany, and a setter he kept in Iowa. I enjoyed the very different aspects of this upland hunting. (The lack of nightlife in What Cheer fitted my style perfectly.) However, critters hell-bent to run away from pointed dogs and when flushed sounded like cackling barnyard chickens struck me as far inferior to quail.

Iowa pheasant hunting did have exciting moments. One afternoon, six roosters flushed, and both Bob and I doubled. Just as I finished reloading, two coyotes that had been stalking the pheasants ran from behind a nearby bush—1½ ounces of #5 shot for each one eliminated them. Four pheasants and two coyotes—not bad for a single point. I must say there were plenty of pheasants in What Cheer; we shot our limit each year.

Most bird hunters develop respect and even love for the quail's genteel behavior. In contrast, it's easy to dislike pheasants because of their ungentlemanly characteristics of running and squawking.

At Indiantown, I have occasionally shot chukar partridges, which had escaped from a client who paid for their release. Chukars behave like quail singles but emit a strong odor. My dogs become especially stylish and intense, quivering with pent-up excitement, when pointing chukar partridges.

I hadn't considered hunting Wilson's snipe until I began hunting near LaBelle. These birds are found in wet areas, especially near a recent burn, but their abundance is variable and difficult to predict. Snipe and quail seasons usually coincide. Since snipe can be hunted while the pointers rest during the midday break, they've become a welcome addition to my hunting activities.

Snipe provide sporty shooting, usually flushing twenty to thirty yards from the hunter, and employ a very irregular flight pattern that make them difficult to hit. When flushed, snipe emit a squawking sound that conveys a tone of derision, a sound guaranteed to disgust and enrage any hunter who has missed ten shots in a row. The best approach to these difficult-to-hit birds is to point and shoot, relying entirely on one's reflexes. When hit, with only a single pellet, snipe almost always come down.

The use of a retriever is essential when hunting snipe. These downed birds can be difficult to find since they frequently fall into thick cover or ponds. Also, when only wounded, they run and hide. One of Joey's Labradors, Champ, a most competent retriever of snipe, had a major (or minor) fault, depending on one's point of view: He always ate two of the birds.

I never anticipated the moment when this malfeasance would occur, but occur it did—invariably. No pantomime artist could have done it better. When Champ returned with a snipe nestled in his mouth, the bird would suddenly disappear. The only evidence implicating Champ was an occasional telltale feather on his lips. I have never seen another dog that, without obvious chewing or some outward sign of swallowing, could engulf a whole bird.

But the show got even better. Champ would top off his slight-of-mouth performance with showmanship, pretending to hunt as if the bird had escaped and fluttered away. If overly admonished to end this farce, the persecuted Champ refused to participate in the retrieving process altogether.

"Why associate with people who don't trust me?" he seemed to say.

Ultimately, I let him eat his two birds. The difference between six and eight snipe is not significant, and they ain't all that tasty, anyway.

Recently I hit a snipe, but while still in the air, it was attacked by a Cooper's hawk. Tar (another Labrador), the snipe, and the hawk all arrived simultaneously at the same spot on the ground. The hawk, executing his plan faster and more efficiently, grabbed the snipe and flew away with Tar in hot, but ineffective, pursuit. I wanted to kid him about being outwitted by a bird, but fearing a sit-down strike, I let it pass.

Potpourri

The section of Florida east of Indiantown is a favorite wintering place for all kinds of migratory avian species, including hawks. A plethora of these raptors present an unwanted predator problem for quail, especially those that are freshly released. On the other hand, they help "educate" the surviving birds to become wild quickly. One of Faith's last points resulted in flushing a hawk with a freshly killed quail in its talons.

There is an ever-present danger from rattlesnakes (eastern diamondback or pygmy) and cottonmouth water moccasins. While hunting, I kill about one poisonous snake every two to three years, but Lib is the only pointer to have been bitten. Unfortunately, the aforementioned Champ tried unsuccessfully to retrieve a large rattlesnake. He did not survive the multiple bites.

The area we hunt contains a number of slews and canals that are havens for fairly large alligators. To date, not one of our dogs has become gator excrement, though Joey did have a small hound dragged under the water by a gator while the dogs were otherwise occupied baying a boar.

Feral hogs can be ferocious and are capable of seriously hurting or killing a bird dog, but so far have not presented a serious problem. The dogs quickly learn to leave them alone. Recently, Tyre came close to a major disaster in an altercation with a hog. I heard him yelp, and he ran to me with a wide, deep cut in the front part of his right shoulder. A few inches higher up in his neck and Tyre would no longer be with us.

For a long period of time, Joey kept the hogs confined in a "hog pen." Unfortunately, the red deer and buffalo learned that abundant feed grain was available in the enclosure and set about destroying the fence. Thus, the hogs now are in great abundance all over the ranch. On rare occasions, one of the bird dogs will point a hog, invariably in a thick place so that the animal is not visible. By far, the best way to distinguish between quail or hog is to rely on the cocker spaniel flush dogs. If they refuse to go into the thick place, it's a hog. Get the hell out of there.

Recently, the presence of water buffalo on the preserve has added another level of excitement. Usually, they hide in thick areas that we avoid; singles that fly into these places are not followed. On occasion, however, the buffalo can act a bit testy, which translates into chasing the dogs and generally making a nuisance of themselves. Although to date, no serious incident has occurred, several episodes need describing.

In 2006, a severe drought occurred, and as a result the birds didn't raise many young. The ones that were there were quite hard to find. Quail adapt to critical situations reasonably well. Most of the remaining coveys occupied the previously water-covered slews, moving into the feeding areas only early in the morning and late in the evening. Frequently, the dogs would follow the birds to these thick areas. Unfortunately, that's also where the "buffalo roam." As a general rule, we were quite careful when following the dogs into these thickets.

One buffalo in particular was a cause of concern. Recently, he had severely hurt his leg and become quite belligerent. (Actually, he caught his foot in his own horn. Although it was successfully extricated, a large necrotic sore developed with the bone showing.) He frequented a particular area, which we avoided. One day, when trailing birds in a slew approximately one-half mile from the bull's usual haunt, I encountered him at close quarters. The distance from the crippled bull to Tyre and me was approximately fifteen feet. To say the least, I felt quite an adrenaline rush. (This feeling was quite similar to a situation at the Zuka Game Ranch in South Africa while I was hunting francolin. As I walked around a bush, I nearly ran into a female rhinoceros with a young calf.) In both situations, luckily, I withdrew without mishap. Tyre also got the message and retreated in good order. Those quail had found themselves an excellent guardian.

Recently, a tranquil morning had an abrupt ending. Ulysses and Tyre slammed on the brakes, each trying to outdo the other in style. The covey flew my way, resulting in a somewhat unusual double, and icing on the cake, a late rising single. After I proclaimed "Dead birds," the dogs started to retrieve. I looked at Joey. He was on the telephone. Usually when he is interrupted while hunting, it's for something important like "Should we have biscuits or rolls for lunch?" At any rate, this time his countenance seemed a little strained.

He called out to me, "We need to get on the swamp buggy, now!"

I stared at him.

"Come on! A client has just wounded a big buffalo. He's headed our way."

In a millisecond the issue was clarified. Dealing with a ton of hurt and mad buffalo with #7½ birdshot ain't likely to be fruitful. I followed after Joey somewhat faster than my usual slovenly pace. From the relatively safe location on the buggy, I breathed a sigh of relief. Both the client and Kevin Roberts, the guide, appeared—following the blood trail. They found where the bull had crossed the canal and had gone into the area where we were hunting, approximately one hundred yards from our location. All of this happened in about five minutes from the time the covey was flushed. We loaded the dogs and went elsewhere. This episode ended without mishap.

They found the bull about sixty or seventy yards farther into the broomstraw, sick and waiting for revenge. They administered a quietus. Lesson learned: I will never complain when Joey answers the telephone while we're quail hunting.

Bird hunting in Florida afforded me another very positive opportunity to expand my butterfly collection. South Florida has a rich population of unique butterflies. I waited to begin this endeavor until I had cemented my relationship with Joey. I didn't want him to conclude that I was a "nut," at least not at the beginning. When I showed up with my butterfly-collecting paraphernalia, I was, as expected, confronted by his incredulous stare . . . complete with eyes rolling heavenward. However, he adapted to the format of my being equipped with butterfly net, as well as shotgun, and actually seemed to enjoy helping out with the proceedings. On several occasions, Joey presented me with "specimens" taken either from the grill of his truck or found dead on the highway. I hated to hurt his feelings, but finally had to tell him that a broken-wing, torn, and bedraggled butterfly didn't add much to my collection.

Joey, however, was less than complimentary when the dogs pointed while I was occupied chasing butterflies. I remember one occasion, when the entire morning had been a water-haul. I spied an unusual specimen (a giant swallowtail), grabbed my net, and was off to the races! Close by, Lib II pointed. Inadvertently, I flushed the covey . . . armed only with the net! Joey and Lib II pouted for the rest of the afternoon.

Hannah curtailed my collecting, perhaps by chance, or by thinking things out. (She had occasional flashes of brilliance.) One day, as I was sneaking up on a newly hatched zebra swallowtail resting on a myrtle bush, she ran by, observed the situation, and decided to participate. She beat me to the butterfly, flushed it, watched it fly off, and resumed hunting. Joey laughed so hard he nearly fell off the buggy. I never have found a better specimen, and vowed never to forgive Hannah for this malfeasance.

Indelible Memories

Reflecting on my hunts for Florida quail, I have concluded that the past two-plus decades have comprised a most enjoyable (and expensive) experience. Every day brings new adventures, too numerous to recount. A few vignettes, however, virtually demand repeating.

While I was still hunting in LaBelle, Joey and I were hunting with four dogs, two more than usual, in a fairly large open field. The dogs converged toward the center from the four points of the compass. When they were approximately fifty yards apart, all four pointed simultaneously, a beautiful, breathtaking sight I doubt I shall ever see repeated.

Although unrelated to bird hunting, the following incident taught me the meaning of the generally accepted origin for the word "cracker" as it pertains to an indigenous citizen of Florida/Georgia. For several years following the move of J&R Outfitters to Indiantown, the quail hunting area contained a fairly large herd of cows owned by one of Joey's close friends. One afternoon while we were hunting, I heard a loud popping sound occurring every minute or so. The source seemed to be moving in our direction, but I couldn't decipher the cause. I queried Joey as to the origin of the noise. He gave me a you-don't-know-much look and indicated that Robert was gathering cows. The noise, caused by cracking a whip, got the cows attention and helped drive them to the desired location. Hence the term "cracker" came into being to designate a local cowboy who cracked a whip. Live and learn.

Dogs often talk to you with their eyes. Times too numerous to count, after a lengthy search for Hannah and finally finding her pointed, I have walked up to her, and she's rolled her eyes at me with a disgusted look, clearly asking, "Where in the world have you been? The birds are still here, thanks to me, but a dog does get tired of standing like this!"

In 1997, hunting near sundown in unfamiliar territory, I released Faith by herself. (Because only one beeper collar was working, I didn't want to risk losing a dog pointing in the dark.) Faith trailed near the truck for a few minutes, then moved about seventy-five yards and pointed. Joey and I followed as she glided rapidly and gracefully forward, back rigid and tail straight, through a pine thicket, an overgrown ditch, and finally into an open weed field—a total distance of some three hundred yards.

Suddenly, Faith planted herself solidly near a covey that was getting ready to roost. I'm certain the birds had not run in front of her; she had winded them at a nearly impossible distance. Such a performance so pumped us with adrenaline that when the covey flushed, I am not sure how we hit anything. Two birds did fall, however, probably perishing from fright.

Did we learn anything about controlling our emotions? No!

Faith gave an encore performance ten days later, this time at the more modest, but still remarkable, distance of one hundred yards, and a large covey flushed. Four shots rang out, shattering the sylvan calm, and all the birds continued to fly away. One must compose one's self, I assume, to shoot straight, right after witnessing greatness.

(I would never want to minimize the talents of the sainted Spot—who along with my father and uncle, made me love this sport—but, truth be told, Faith had skills superior to any bird dog I have owned or seen. Although Faith frequently was a pain in the ass, she remains unmatched.)

A striking difference between Florida quail and their larger cousins in the upper South is their propensity to run. This modus operandi of escape is used most frequently when ground cover is sparse, e.g., in a recently burned field.

Occasionally, a covey may be spotted running along a grass-covered dike beside a canal. Handling a situation like this is difficult for a bird dog; the temptation to chase and flush is almost overwhelming. It takes an outstanding bird dog to handle running quail. The dog must follow closely enough so that the birds do not run away and escape, yet not push so rapidly that they flush. If pursued properly, the birds usually stop in the first significant cover they come to and hold for a point.

Anne, Hannah, Faith, and, more recently, Horatio have developed the knack of handling running quail. An additional advantage of hustling behind dogs so engaged is guaranteed to produce an optimal cardiac stress test. It has helped me to be certain I don't have coronary artery disease.

A recent, spectacular episode involving Horatio and running birds must be documented. He followed the hustling covey for nearly one hundred yards to the edge of a drainage canal, which was twenty feet wide and containing water about four feet deep, and came to a staunch point. The birds had fluttered across. While maintaining a rigid pose, Horatio eased into the water, both head and tail up, and slowly swam across. Arriving at the other side and still pointing, he slowly climbed halfway up the bank. He froze, pointing the bevy huddled under a myrtle bush. What a spectacular sight—pointing while swimming—a sight not seen by me before, and, undoubtedly, I never will again.

Recently, one evening as the twilight shadows advanced and birds were moving, Lou and Jeb pointed. Two birds fell following the rise of a small covey. Both Lou and Jeb grabbed a bird and started to retrieve. Suddenly, both turned and simultaneously pointed the remainder of the broken covey, each having a bird in its mouth. It's difficult to grade spectacular sights, but this clearly was a ten.

Early one morning, we were hunting through an area covered with cabbage palms and thick palmettos where a number of single birds had flown. As I walked to the other side of the thicket, I spied both Ulysses and Scylla on point, about fifteen yards in front of me. Just as I saw them, a very large turkey gobbler with an impressive beard became airborne and flew within easy gun range, even for #7½ shot. Remembering that Joey collected $1500 for an Osceola gobbler from turkey hunters trying to obtain a "Grand Slam," I didn't shoot. (The Osceola turkey has a very restricted range and is highly coveted.)

As I watched this beautiful, impressive bird fly into the distance, landing about five hundred yards away, I suddenly noticed that both Scylla and Ulysses were still on point. One more step forward and the remnants of the covey flushed. While two of these birds were retrieved, I couldn't help but conclude, "quail trumps turkeys" every time. Reflecting on these and myriad other wonderful memories, I am really appreciative of every day the Good Lord allows me to hunt quail with pointer bird dogs.

Tiny

Ten years ago, Tiny came into my life:
Thirty-five pounds of half-trained strife.
She would not back, had a second-rate nose.
Why I kept her, God only knows.
Right from the start it was easy to see
A desire to please and untiring energy.
She was seldom first on a covey find,
But retrieving birds she learned to shine.
When the covey explodes and "dead bird" is called,
At work Tiny stays till she finds them all.
No cripple can hide or successfully roam

When the ground is covered with her fine-toothed comb.
Head cocked to the left she circles around,
Through briars, palmettos or muddy ground.
Ponds or streams can't stop her drive
To bring in the bird—but not alive.
With a bird in her mouth she trots to me,
And proudly shows off for all to see.
I will admit when the bird is dressed,
A few tooth marks are on the breast.
When searching for a cripple becomes a bore,
And the rest of the dogs won't hunt any more,
Exasperated you'll hear me shout,
"Go to the truck; turn Tiny out."
As the years roll on, someday it will end.
But for now she's Queen of the pen.
Run and hunt with a cracking tail,
And bring in cripples when the others fail.
(1992)

Hannah

Ghosting ahead at a ground-eating pace,
A faint perfume strikes her full in the face.
Whirling to the right to test the air,
Ten more steps—she knows they are there.
She points—head up—a ballet dance,
Eyes unfocused, as if in a trance.
Still as death, not moving a hair
Until the covey explodes in the air.
Shots ring out; one drops in flight.
Reluctantly, she brings the bird to sight.
Eager to move on and resume her quest,
Another covey, to be first and best.
Why does she hunt through heat and rain?
Certainly not for her master's gain.
Only to prove when the big dogs run,
She'll not be beaten by anyone.
(1994)

Anne

To look at Anne you would never guess
That she was counted among the best.
A body too long with low-set tail
Didn't stop her from finding quail.
Dish-faced, one-eye, overshot jaws,
Pockmarked skin, splayed-out paws.
Handicaps Anne would overcome
By the drive in her heart to point and run.
Yes, Anne was ugly when in the pen,
But in the field she'd always win.
One quality carried her above the rest:
An enduring will to be the best.
(1995)

Faith

A dish-faced puppy, not much to see,
Faith looked like an early cull to me.
But from the start, unlike the others
Her nose led her from one bird to another.
By age two Faith outbirded the rest,
But her main goal was to be a pest.
Fight, self-hunt, infrequently back,
Only her nose kept her from the sack.
When finally she lost those "demons from hell,"
Hunting with Faith has been a delight to tell.
Both Sage grouse and quail she points quite well
From scent so faint only she can smell.
Faith winds birds a quarter-mile with ease
And follows running coveys till they stop and freeze.
When the other dogs falter, Joey will grunt,
"Little Black Death should join the hunt."
(1998)

Between Scylla And Charybdis

Neither monster nor a maelstrom,
But a pair of pointer dogs
Who search the fields for Bobwhite quail
Through dry land and through bogs.
No matter how well the birds can hide
So the dogs run by and miss,
They'll soon be held by stylish points
Between Scylla and Charybdis.
(2006)

Jeb

What words describe big Jeb the best?
Staunch on point and picturesque,
Running big with speed an style,
Retrieving birds—but, never alive.
Sire of pups, the best no doubt.
Bark in the truck 'till he's turned out.
To tell the truth, when all's said and done,
One-eyed Jeb was a lot of fun.
(2007)

To Horatio: On His 12th Birthday

Like Caesar, Horatio
Was born to this life's wheel.
Bottle-fed by me until
Missy, his mother, could heal.
Named for characters of
Shakespearian acclaim,
This star-crossed litter of puppies
Was destined for future fame.
While out alone he trained himself
To hunt both true and fast.
He learned where quail could be found
To point with style and class.
For ten great years Horatio
Was the best of the best.
Pointing coveys and singles—
Always ahead of the rest.
As the sands of time run down,
He's grown deaf and frail.
But by God's eternal grace
He still finds Bobwhite quail.
Soon Horatio will join Spot,
Rena, Faith and Hannah.
And hunt with them for coveys
In Heaven's celestial savannah.
Made weak by time and fate,
His earthly quest must end.
I salute you, staunch Horatio. . . .
As a bird dog and my friend.
(2008)

Why Hunt Birds?

Chapter VI

I have posed this question to myself on numerous occasions. This is especially true when I'm exhausted at the end of a long day and I arrive back at the truck with the seat of my pants ripped open by a barbed-wire fence and my body severely lacerated from an encounter with cat-claw briars and covered with mud and slime from falling into a well-disguised bog.

I have asked this question most poignantly when having to kill an old or disabled dog that I have loved and hunted with for years. Even when everything has gone well, there remains in my mind questions about the sanity of this avocation. Why hunt birds?

I have no ready answer, though two are frequently cited by participants as being important: healthy exercise and putting meat on the table. I must say that neither of those reasons has the slightest bearing on why I hunt birds. Although bird hunting does, indeed, require considerable walking, a more vigorous and less time-consuming method of exercising may be achieved with an exercise bicycle. Also, the mental strain and loss of voice that results from dealing with obstreperous pointers cannot be considered healthy. Further, the concept of bird hunting to provide cheap table fare is really ludicrous. My cost last year—approximately eighty dollars per bird—hardly qualifies as inexpensive food. Granted that quail may be delicious to many; the fact is, I prefer chicken.

The sport of bird hunting may be divided into three components: bird shooting, bird dogs and shotguns. Perhaps the lure of bird hunting can be found by examining the relative interest in each component by several groups of people generally classified (either by themselves or their friends) as bird hunters: 1) general outdoorsmen, 2) shooters, 3) the field trial fraternity, 4) dog owners, 5) gun collectors, and finally, 6) the true bird hunters. What follows describes the salient features of each of these groups.

General outdoorsmen view bird hunting as just one component in a long list of sporting activities including hunting upland game, waterfowl, and big game . . . as well as playing golf, skiing, and chasing women. These types commit to all these activities in various proportions, the latter usually predominating. Big-game hunting provides the added opportunity to collect trophies (the stuffed body parts of animals or the whole animal itself) with which to clutter up the house. General outdoorsmen enjoy the camaraderie of a variety of sports, especially drinking and bragging. Bird hunting, thus, is only a minor part of their total sporting experience. They are unlikely to concern themselves with high-quality dog work or owning a fine shotgun.

Shooters, the second category, have a built-in need to kill a large quantity of game, and they are not happy if they don't. By nature, shooters are very competitive and consider bird hunting a sport in which the person who kills the most birds is declared the winner. Shooters may be readily identified by the first question they invariably ask regarding a hunt: "How many birds did you get?" Unfortunately, most bird hunters I have met in recent years fall into this category. They are often good shots, since their thrill is killing birds, but they have no hesitation in emptying a five-shot automatic every time a covey rises. The current plethora of bird hunting preserves depend on these individuals for clients; at ten dollars a bird, forty to fifty birds amounts to a tidy tab.

When discussing bird hunting, shooters expound on the pleasure the performance of high-quality dogs gives them. However, if asked for particulars of the dog work prior to or during the covey rise, it becomes obvious that they have no notion of whether the dogs were even in the same county. Shooters may pose a serious threat to a bird dog's well being. I've had two superb pointers killed and several more wounded by shooters hell-bent to kill a low flying quail—the dog be damned. (Personally, I would like to evoke the Code of Hammurabi in dealing with these trigger-happy dolts.) Finally, shooters regard a shotgun as a useful tool, never as a work of art.

The field trial community, the third category, enjoys the competition of field trials and watching bird dogs perform. A significant variation in participation exists, ranging from very rich people who vicariously enjoy paying a trainer loads of money to campaign a dog they own but rarely see (occasionally they get pieces of inscribed metal defining a dog's exploits), to sportsmen who train and handle their own dogs. Both professional and amateur trainers are often dedicated and knowledgeable individuals who expend enormous amounts of energy developing dogs with the skills needed to win field trials. But here's the rub: The characteristics that win field trials do not necessarily define an excellent bird-hunting dog.

Field trial competition varies from open-all-age (one is lucky even to keep up with the dog while riding a fast racehorse), to shoot-to-retrieve competitions that theoretically simulate bird hunting. I have attended a number of the "bird-hunting" type of trials. Usually confusion seems to prevail, with dogs running willy-nilly, paying little attention to cover and finally traversing a "bird field" in which birds are scattered without any regard for whether the location appears natural. Unfortunately, I have purchased several pointers that competed effectively in shoot-to-retrieve trials but proved to be incompetent at actually finding and pointing wild birds. Fine shotguns obviously play no part in field trials.

A very positive aspect of field trials is that dogs that are bred to perform in major competition have maintained the style and hunting drive of the English pointer. My hat is off to the responsible breeders and trainers.

Our fourth category, dog owners, consists of those interested primarily in exercising their dogs. Hunting is not part of their makeup. But they have either purchased or been given a bird dog (often a Brittany, Irish setter, or some other fuzzy breed) and have become quite attached to their family companion. Reading the description of their dog, provided by the American Kennel Club, they have concluded that it should be hunted. Thus, dog owners are tramping the woods to exercise their pets and help them maintain healthy bowel habits. Again, fine shotguns are not part of the scenario.

Gun collectors or "gun nuts," depending on your point of view, comprise the fifth category. They avidly seek and acquire fine shotguns and are enthralled by the feel of a custom double. Although they try their treasures occasionally in a hunting venue, they have only a remote interest in bird hunting and bird dogs. To them, owning the shotgun is what counts, not hunting.

True bird hunters (at most, two percent) make up the final group. Those in this group consider the addicting avocation of bird hunting to be nothing less than the key to the enjoyment of life. From late November until early March, the everyday problems of life become unimportant. Quail season is open! Each component of bird hunting—birds, dogs, shotguns—combine in changing proportions to paint a beautiful canvas.

Havilah Babcock eloquently characterized the seasonal salutary effect of quail hunting in *My Health is Better in November*. Personally, I would invert this statement and say, My health goes to hell in March! Both my physical and mental well-being remains decidedly subpar until the first covey rise in the fall.

Dyed-in-the-wool bird hunters frequently choose to hunt by themselves. My primary reason for hunting with others is that they own the land and have invited me to participate. Without them there would be no hunt. Except for this eminently cogent reason, I am at a loss to understand why one would hunt with a companion.

A major drawback inherent in hunting with someone else is the risk of having some portion of your anatomy or, more importantly, your dog's anatomy, rearranged by a trigger-happy partner. The risk of being shot is not nearly as annoying as being told at 4:00 P.M., just when birds are starting to move, that your companion has a 6:00 P.M. dinner engagement, and his spouse will be angry as hell if he is not on time. When all is said and done, I'm happier when hunting alone.

In this respect I differ from many bird hunters, including Havilah Babcock who describes the reasons for companionship while bird hunting in *I Don't Want to Shoot an Elephant*. Obviously, if two dedicated bird hunters are compatible and enjoy hunting together, that's fine. But, two should be the limit; three or more hunters increase the danger exponentially.

Unless physically unable, the true bird hunter will choose to hunt wild quail. This endeavor will entail either many hours of fruitless searching or else taking part in an extraordinarily expensive endeavor. Certainly there are many shooting preserves that make a considerable effort to simulate wild-bird hunting. Undoubtedly, for some, recently released birds may serve as a reasonable substitute for wild birds. But, and it is a very big but, not for me or for other dyed-in-the-wool bird hunters. Wild, or thoroughly acclimated, quail in their natural habitat are the necessary game.

The love of bird dogs, the second component in the triad, is essential for the true bird hunter. The English pointer is the overwhelming choice in the Deep South. The dedicated bird hunter always looks after his own dogs. He insists on high-quality dog work and is not satisfied unless the dogs perform to a very high standard.

Lastly, true bird hunters admire fine shotguns. It goes without saying that their choice will be a double barrel. What kind of double barrel? I think if God believed that an over-and-under were superior to a side-by-side, He would have placed our eyes in a different configuration! I do grudgingly admit that using an over-and-under does not automatically disqualify an individual from being a member of the select few. This is certain: The pride in using a custom double shotgun is a major part of the true bird hunter's enjoyment.

Why hunt birds? The simple answer is that nothing, absolutely nothing, beats watching a pair of pointers cover a picturesque piece of ground in a workmanlike manner and slamming on brakes to a stylish point. Or an even better answer might be that nothing beats admiring your pointers as they precisely handle a running covey. This tableau, immediately followed by the feel of a fine double shotgun brought into play, and accompanied by the thunderous sound of the covey flushing is an experience without equal. There may be a few things I haven't tried, but nothing I have attempted, seen, or read about even comes close.

Shooting Quail—A Primer

Chapter VII

Let's define an excellent bird shot as a hunter who averages killing one bird from each covey rise and 50 percent of the singles at which he shoots. If the hunting venue is open terrain, like low bush-palmettos in Florida, the average should be better. When shooting in second growth pine or honeysuckle thickets in North Carolina, scores will be worse. To achieve this level of success, two basic skills need mastering: 1) familiarity and competence with a shotgun and 2) the ability to shut out distractions and concentrate on killing quail.

Early in life I was indoctrinated to believe that a side-by-side double-barrel shotgun was the only appropriate weapon with which to hunt birds. I have never questioned the wisdom of this premise nor tried an alternative. My use of a double, then, rests on tradition and not first-hand knowledge of the alternatives. Numerous articles and books have been penned by a variety of experts regarding the proper choice of a shotgun, and I cannot exceed their sagacity. Suffice to say that, if the only goal is to kill quail, any shotgun that fits the shooter should be adequate.

I started hunting with a 20-gauge Parker that belonged to my grandfather, and with it I became reasonably proficient. About age forty I began wounding too many birds but, being a slow learner, it took me until age forty-five to realize I needed a denser pattern and more shot. I've used a 12-gauge ever since.

When I first used a 20-gauge, the standard shell contained $^7/_8$ of an ounce of shot. The 12-gauge shells with which I currently hunt have either 1 ounce or $1^1/_8$ ounces of shot. The recent trend to increase the number of shot in a 20-gauge shell has essentially turned the 20 into a 12. However, the "souped-up" 20 won't pattern as well as the 12 because the shot string is longer. Contrary to the opinion of numerous outdoor sports mavens, it is not more sporting to use a 20-gauge.

The shotgun for upland gunning should be fairly light. Why be weighted-down by a gun you can't point rapidly? The one I use weighs six pounds, four ounces, just right for me, and not much heavier than many 20-gauge shotguns.

Professionals who make their living shooting in international skeet, sporting clays, and trap competitions, or on the live pigeon circuit, generally advise using a heavy gun. No doubt these well-trained athletes do quite well killing quail with a 7½-pound or heavier shotgun. They have the speed and strength to point quickly and shoot a heavier gun, even in thick cover. However, as one grows older and reflexes slow, a lighter gun is a better choice. The slightly increased kick from a lighter gun won't matter with the number of shots likely to be fired when hunting birds but is of major importance when the shooter expends two to three hundred shells a day in competition. Regarding choke—it's hard to beat improved cylinder.

Become thoroughly familiar with your shotgun. In my opinion, this is the primary secret to successful bird shooting; pointing and shooting should become a second-nature reflex.

Nowadays, the amount of practice required to excel isn't likely to be gained in actual hunting where opportunities are limited. I recommend a hand trap or another device that throws skeet. Once the hunter can break 90 percent of the skeet thrown at all angles, he'll be skilled enough to kill birds.

The brand of shotgun shells is not critical. They shouldn't be the cheapest on the market that contain soft, easily deformable shot, which results in a poor pattern and mediocre penetration. Choose shells with hard shot. Although quail can be killed with shot sizes ranging from 6 to 9, I've settled on 7½. A standard field load has plenty of powder; maximum load or high brass shells aren't needed.

Concentrate on killing the quail. Along with many dedicated bird hunters, I find this incredibly difficult. I am so entranced watching the dogs point and enjoying the entire spectacle that my mind drifts away from the task at hand—killing birds. On many occasions, the birds fly off without my having the presence of mind to shoot. Thus, if one's sole goal is to kill birds, paying attention to other aspects of the hunting experience can be a hindrance. At any rate, what follows are a few observations I hope may help place the hunter in the best situation to make those killing shots.

A bird hunter should consider quail as having the attributes of a gentleman unwillingly participating in the sport. The quail deserves every courtesy, including that of a clean kill. It should go without saying that quail must be shot only while on the wing. Ground shooting is the moral equivalent of stealing from the church collection plate . . . or worse.

Successful shooting begins with a correct approach to the pointing dogs. Move toward the dogs from either their side or the rear. This approach usually allows the hunter to be in front of the dogs when the covey flushes, thereby avoiding shooting directly over their heads.

Despite opinions to the contrary, quail cannot be driven in a preferred direction. Wild birds fly where they damn well want to fly, usually to favorite cover. In thick cover they seem to have an uncanny ability to interpose a bush or sapling between themselves and the hunter as they execute their escape. Therefore, a hunter should survey the terrain, identify the likely escape route, and try to position himself for an unobstructed shot after the flush.

The hunter should walk to the pointing dogs at a reasonably brisk gait, keeping his eyes focused in front of the dog, not on the ground. Never try to spot quail on the ground. (In my experience, if I see a bird on the ground, that bird, when flushed, invariably will be missed.)

When the covey flushes, the hunter should be well balanced and optimally positioned to shoot. If he is right-handed, the left foot should be slightly in front and the body weight shifted forward to enable an easy pivot in either direction. As the hunter nears the covey, taking short steps facilitates good balance and allows him to quickly assume the correct shooting position.

The gun should be carried with the butt below the armpit and the muzzle pointing approximately 45 degrees upward. Actually, shooting will be more accurate if the muzzle is pointed in a downward direction. When it is brought up to point at the bird, the gun's momentum follows in the correct direction since the bird is usually rising. Conversely, with the muzzle up, the momentum carries the gun in precisely the wrong direction.

Most birds flying directly away from the hunter are missed by undershooting, and, thus, the argument is made for carrying the shotgun with the muzzle pointed down. But, and this is a huge but, the problem with carrying the gun with the muzzle down is that if the hunter prematurely discharges the weapon, he may very well blow off the dog's head. Forget any notion of walking with the muzzle down.

If nothing has happened after moving twenty or thirty feet in front of the pointing dogs, stop and have the dogs relocate and point. If the birds are running, both hunter and dogs must follow fairly rapidly. The goal is not only to move the dogs fast enough so the birds can't escape but also to prevent them from flushing the birds.

When the covey flushes, if possible, the hunter should try to kill the first bird off the ground. If the bird doesn't fall, shoot again. On the other hand, if the bird does go down and the hunter feels compelled to shoot again, he has plenty of time to pick out a second bird. Good hunters avoid shooting into the middle of a covey. They pick out birds on the periphery. The scarcity of wild quail makes it mandatory not to shoot into a covey and risk wounding several birds.

The appropriate time to shoot after the birds have flushed has been dealt with by numerous writers, both expert hunters and those sedentary sages who make a living writing "how-to-shoot" articles. To profit from these instructors, the reader ought to consider whether he has the same physical and mental makeup as the author. For instance, it was entirely reasonable for Nash Buckingham (*Mark Right)*, an accomplished athlete who shot thousands of quail, to admonish hunters not to shoot too fast and thus miss or disintegrate the bird. Buckingham's "repression technique" involved waiting for the covey to get sufficiently airborne before picking out a bird and shouldering the shotgun.

Again, this advice is well and good if your reflexes are as fast as his. Mine aren't! Under normal circumstances, as soon as I can point and squeeze the trigger, the bird will be at an appropriate killing distance. Using this approach, no doubt I have disintegrated a few birds at close range, but shooting and wounding the majority at thirty or thirty-five yards has been avoided.

Besides age and congenital slowness, I am further handicapped by hearing difficulties. I didn't realize the importance this sense plays in locating flushed birds until I became nearly deaf in my right ear and lost the ability to pinpoint the direction of sound. The loss of hearing in that ear happened abruptly in 1985. Except for difficulty discriminating among sounds, my ability to hear previously had been excellent. One day, sitting under a tree still-hunting squirrels, I heard one bark. Try as I might, I couldn't locate the squirrel by sound. I finally spotted him on a limb of the very tree that I was sitting under. I quickly determined that I had become nearly deaf in my right ear. An audiologist confirmed my observation, and a medical workup ruled out a brain tumor, relieving my anxiety. Still, I was deaf in one ear. Over the ensuing years, except for hunting, I have made this handicap an advantage, turning my "deaf ear" toward people I want to ignore.

To return to the subject, the way to determine the proper time to shoot after the birds have flushed is to judge correctly one's own capabilities. For me, the hardest bird to hit is one that flies directly away. I often undershoot by failing to account for the fact that the bird is generally rising. A rising bird needs to be covered by the muzzle when the shot is taken.

A flushed bird that flies directly over the hunter is also difficult to hit. Usually the hunter must turn around and find the bird again before shooting. If a hunter is right-handed, the easiest bird to hit is one flying to his left. This bird stays in range for a longer time, and the gun's right-to-left movement is natural. Contrarily, birds flying from left to right are harder to kill. When the hunter swings the shotgun to the right, he often drops (rainbows) the muzzle and undershoots.

Whether the bird flies to the left or right, the hunter should move the muzzle along the plane of the bird's flight and take the shot as the muzzle passes the bird. Frankly, when I am functioning correctly, I'm totally unaware of everything except pointing the gun and the bird falling.

The instant the gun is empty, reload and be ready to shoot again. (It's not uncommon when the covey flushes for one or two birds to sit and flush late.) Many times in close cover, the hunter can't determine whether the bird has been hit the instant the gun is fired. Even if certain the bird has been missed, hunt the dogs in the direction the birds were flying. I have been amazed the number of times a dog has found an unsuspected dead bird a hundred yards or more from the point of flush.

To reiterate, the key to killing birds from a covey rise is to pick out one bird and make sure you kill it. Strangely, most hunters shoot less well on coveys than on singles, probably because of excitement generated by the covey rise and the difficulty in picking out one bird. On the other hand, a hunter who grows blasé to the thrill of a covey rise should switch to bungee jumping. No, even that would not help. Nothing can rekindle the spirit of such a citizen.

If it is clear that flushed birds will fly over a pond or thick marsh where it will be impossible to retrieve them, it is best not to shoot. If the hunter follows this advice, but the dog expects shooting as a reward for his efforts, my advice is to discharge the gun and mutter a favorite profanity; thus, communicating a miss to the dog.

On a given day, how many birds from a covey should be killed? My personal limit is one per covey rise and one single. This way a covey can be hunted two or three times without being decimated. Frequently a bird with only a broken wing will dive to the ground and appear to be quite dead. Unless you know the bird has been killed outright, have the dog locate the quail as soon as possible to avoid letting the bird have time to run off.

When hunting released birds, especially those that have been in the field for only a short period of time, the sport changes markedly. For example, because of lack of oil on their feathers, released quail become waterlogged, especially early in the morning, and they have a hard time getting airborne. An instinctive bird shooter will hesitate, then delay too long; often the birds will be out of range when he finally fires.

Newly released birds know nothing about cover; they fly willy-nilly in any direction. The hunter trying to figure an escape route is wasting time. They fly over bushes and other obstructions, rather than through them, as do wild quail. When pen-raised birds flush, they frequently alight after traveling only a few yards. This is danger time. Bird dogs in the vicinity can be shot. One of my favorite bird dogs, Fanny, was killed by one of Joey's trigger-happy clients who shot at a short-flighted bird. Recently, the irreplaceable Hamlet met a similar fate.

Additionally, a quick-witted bird dog may actually catch slow-flying released birds in the air, making it mandatory when pulling the trigger that the only thing in the pattern is the bird. In my opinion, the sole reason for training a bird dog to be steady to wing and shot is to avoid the danger inherent in an erratic and brief flight pattern.

All the preceding advice is predicated on the notion that you hunt by yourself. For me, hunting with someone else usually detracts from the enjoyment, but this belief places me in a minority. Most quail hunters prefer companionship, and that's fine, but they should realize that they have increased the danger to themselves and their friends.

Rules must be established before two or more hunters go into the field. It should be crystal clear who will shoot at which bird and that no shot will ever be taken in the direction of the other hunter. The hunter on the right (approaching the pointing dogs) shoots birds that fly to the right; his partner shoots those moving left. Occasionally both may double on the same bird as it flies to the front, but it is not acceptable to crossfire into the other hunter's territory. For the uninitiated, quail hunting can be quite dangerous. If people must hunt together, make two the limit. Any more can be a deadly combination.

It is necessary at all times to know where your partner is. For some reason, a novice approaching pointing dogs assumes that he should stalk the dogs and, thus, moves forward very slowly, as if emulating Daniel Boone. This individual invariably falls behind as you move forward toward the dogs, and suddenly the back of your head becomes an excellent target for his load of shot. If, in spite of repeated requests to keep up, your partner continues to lag, fall on the ground and feign a seizure. It may save your life. Don't count on hollow promises. Don't believe him if he says, "I won't shoot unless a bird flies my way."

When a covey flushes, most people are seized by temporary insanity and do things they later vehemently deny having done. Assuming you have been killed, you won't be in a position to refute their versions. Especially dangerous is shooting at singles the dog hasn't pointed. For example, a bird flushing between two hunters and flying to the rear is always best left for another day. More advice: If your partner shoots at a bird flying over your head, depart. Leave the scene. Run away. Don't even wait for your partial deafness to recede. Your companion is a trigger-happy madman who may add you to his trophy collection.

Safety when using a firearm should always be of paramount importance. One of the cardinal rules of bird hunting is to know exactly where you are shooting and at what you are shooting. The importance of this maxim was indelibly imprinted on me at a young age. I began hunting gray squirrels in the woods near my home with a .22 rifle when I was about eight years old. On the midwinter day in question I had had no luck; in fact, I hadn't even seen a squirrel. Although I had been told on multiple occasions not to shoot into a squirrel nest, I broke the rule. After my shot, nothing happened. I spied a vine hanging down from the nest and gave it a jerk. Much to my surprise, two dead squirrels tumbled out. Without the presence of the handy vine, I never would have known I had killed them. I quit hunting and trudged home with the squirrels, very much ashamed of my performance. I never shot into a squirrel nest after that time.

More particularly, I have been very careful to be certain that when I squeeze the trigger, the resulting pellets or bullet cannot inadvertently cause trouble. (Undoubtedly, the best way to learn is to make a mistake, observe the results, and never repeat the action. Unfortunately, in dealing with gun safety, the initial error may produce fatal results.) At any rate, on this particular afternoon, I learned a very good lesson.

I hope these musings help readers not only improve their marksmanship while quail hunting but also participate in this great sport safely by providing a framework for them. Regarding shooting, I must confess my current skills are too embarrassing to document. Whether this is a temporary slump or a permanent fixture remains to be seen. Regardless, I've convinced myself that killing quail constitutes only a minor part in the overall adventure of bird hunting. Feel free to use the "minor part" excuse to salvage a bruised ego when you shoot poorly!

Can Released Quail Simulate Bird Hunting?

Chapter VIII

For an avid bird hunter whose experiences have been restricted to hunting wild quail, the initial exposure to released quail is invariably disappointing. I am no exception. Although several acquaintances tried to convince me hunting released birds was fun, I remained skeptical and did not participate until one of my patients insisted I try hunting on his brother's preserve. The wild bird season hadn't opened, but bird hunting the year before had been just awful, with no quail, plus a plague of deer hunters. A new approach might be warranted, I told myself, and decided to give released birds a try. The fact that the excursion was free undoubtedly provided an additional attraction.

On the appointed day I arrived about 10:00 A.M. at the preserve, some fifteen miles from my home, accompanied by Pepper. The gracious owner told me that he had just released a dozen birds in a five-acre field reserved for my use. When hunting, Pepper was fairly wide-ranging but easily controlled on singles, so I anticipated no problem keeping him in the designated area. Several other parties hunted close-by on similar-size tracts.

Pepper pointed shortly after we started. I walked in front of him. Nothing happened. Looking down at my feet, I saw a befuddled quail staring up at me in wonderment. I kicked at the forlorn bird, and it flew about three feet, squealed, and landed before I shouldered my gun. Pepper, observing the proceedings, undoubtedly thought the bird was wounded and promptly retrieved it. A great beginning—one bird in the bag and not a shot fired!

I found one quail stretched out on the ground, head under his wing, just as he had been left by the preserve's owner—a sight that contributed to a largely disheartening experience. (Apparently this method of releasing birds kept them from wandering off the small field.) Pepper seemed unenthusiastic regarding released birds, showing considerably less style than when hunting wild singles. As a matter of fact, I couldn't tell if he were pointing or answering a call of nature.

The rest of the hunt consisted of variations on the same uninspiring theme. All the birds were singles, and about two-thirds actually flew, taking a long time to get airborne but proceeding quite competently thereafter. Their flight patterns were unusual, i.e., they did not try to reach any particular cover. Also, they flew much higher than wild birds.

When the wild quail season opened, it became apparent that coveys numbered markedly fewer than even the year before, and, although occasional flights of woodcock provided some sport, I feared my best bird hunting was behind me. In addition, the number of deer in my bird-hunting venues had greatly increased, attracting a number of orange-clad "gentlemen" who wandered around in various stages of inebriation and armed with either shotguns loaded with buckshot or high-powered rifles. Neither my bird dogs nor I resembled a deer, but I was quite dubious if our looks would afford us any protection from these nimrods. Although I vowed not to let the deer hunters scare me off, common sense prevailed, and I curtailed my trips. The dearth of wild birds also played a part in my trying released birds again.

I visited several other preserves, with birds being released just prior to my arrival, either as singles or three to four in a small covey. On occasion the quail flew reasonably well, especially if I waited until late afternoon when the dew had evaporated from their feathers. But, try as I might, I couldn't persuade myself that this bore even a passing resemblance to wild bird hunting. I went back to hunting woodcock, covered from head to toe in blaze orange clothing and talking loudly to myself.

Things didn't improve the next year, 1985. There were fewer quail and more deer hunters. I looked forward to my yearly trip to Florida, but that too proved disappointing. Birds were scarce, and I finally wound up on a preserve near Labelle, part of a sixteen thousand acre farm. The preserve occupied one thousand acres; the rest remained unhunted.

On the eve before a hunt, quail were released in coveys of ten to twelve. Considerable care had been taken to place food (milo or cracked corn) and water in good cover. The legal limit for wild quail in Florida applied on this preserve.

The coveys were scattered over a fairly wide area, and the release points rotated so that the dogs couldn't learn the precise location of the birds. (When feeders are used to attract quail, most pointers figure out the location, race from feeder to feeder, and eschew hunting the intervening territory.)

Clearly, much greater effort was taken to simulate wild-bird hunting than I had seen previously; however, considerable differences still existed between these released birds and their wild counterparts. Perhaps 5 percent of the released birds were squealers. The remainder flushed, but in a manner different from wild quail: They did not flush in unison, nor did they try to escape toward dense cover.

Their initial flight after the flush was slower and, frankly, I found them more difficult to hit. The slower initial flying speed caused me to hesitate, thereby interfering with my standard point-and-shoot technique. Worse, I couldn't concentrate. I was behaving like a bird dog trained on wild birds having to hunt released ones: I had no style. Another drawback was the fact that the birds usually were found close to the release point, so the opportunity was lost to see and enjoy the dogs trail and, especially, follow running quail.

When quail are released as I've described, a significant number will escape the hunter. One might assume that with adequate feed, water, and protection from predators they should acclimate and survive. But, as numerous studies have documented, such is not the case. The vast majority weaken after a few days and perish. Those that do make it (about 5 percent) for a couple of months grow "street smart" and become essentially wild. An attrition rate of this magnitude markedly limits the use of this approach to provide a reasonable facsimile of wild-bird hunting.

How can some of the problems associated with released birds be overcome? An obvious failing is the frequency with which only a partial flush occurs. The result: Several birds fly only a short distance or not at all, running around with all the dignity of a lost barnyard chicken.

This hindrance to hunting enjoyment can be overcome by having the dogs run up the birds on command, but this approach carries a big risk. I've seen only a few pointers that, when assigned this task, haven't been essentially ruined for wild quail. Unfortunately, they become far too aggressive. Released birds have a much greater tolerance than wild birds do for crowding; thus, the dogs quickly became useful for preserve duties only.

To solve this problem, bird dogs can be trained to be steady to wing, and a flushing dog, e.g., an aggressive Labrador retriever or a cocker spaniel, may be used to put the birds in the air. Actually, when hunting wild birds, I have never been a proponent of having a dog steady to wing and shot because a dog so trained is difficult to move when wild quail are running. Obviously, if wild quail are the game, a flush dog is not needed. Flushing the birds with a spaniel while the bird dogs remain pointed has a major added advantage. If one of the birds flushes and immediately drops (i.e., a squealer), a pointer allowed to chase will be on the bird in a heartbeat. A trigger-happy shooter could severely injure or kill the dog.

In the last four to five years, game fowl breeders have made a concerted effort to dramatically enhance the wild nature of quail. Breeders have developed techniques in which the birds are flighted in large pens and are not allowed to become familiar with humans. Only minimum de-beaking is undertaken, which gives the bird, if not killed immediately, a better chance to survive in the wild. A marked improvement also has taken place in the quality of the breeding stock. No doubt, enhancing the wild nature of released birds is a fertile field for research, which will improve the quality of pen-raised birds. Nonetheless, recently released birds have a long way to go before they provide a hunting experience nearly as exciting as wild quail.

A question facing preserve owners and game-fowl breeders is whether to expend the effort and money to improve the quality of released birds. Generally, the shooting public either cannot tell the difference between released and wild quail or have decided to be tolerant.

At a preserve recently, I was surprised at the reaction when the quail released were very sporty, i.e., they flew like wild birds. A number of people complained about the birds being difficult to hit. Fewer birds were killed, and the owner's revenue declined—an outcome I am sure he found unacceptable.

Most hunting preserves in the eastern part of the country seem to do quite well. They function as retreats for wealthy shooters primarily interested in fine accommodations, five-star food, concomitant sporting clays, and the chance to kill (at ten dollars apiece) as many birds as they want. There are numerous such preserves, evidently flourishing. But wild quail hunting it ain't! No matter how I feel, the future of quail hunting depends on pen-raised birds. I hope that everyone involved will strive mightily to make released-bird hunting as close to the real thing as possible.

Scenting Conditions and Bird Hunting

Chapter IX

The most mediocre bird dog, obviously, can outperform any human in perceiving scent. A pointer can detect the faint odor from a nearby bird or, even more remarkably, where a bird has walked in the recent past and follow the trail. He will not only follow, but also know when to slam on the brakes and point before getting too close and flushing the covey. To a man with only a rudimentary sense of smell, this performance seems miraculous.

The ability to perceive scent correctly is even more amazing when one considers the ritual that pointers (at least mine) engage in at the beginning of each hunt. They will find a rotten, dead animal or some other disgusting refuse and roll around in it until they "stink to high heaven" as far as human olfactory sense is concerned, yet they will remain effective in carrying out their bird-finding chores.

Often a hunting venue known to contain several coveys may be thoroughly covered without the dogs finding anything. The next day, however, the birds may be located easily. It is apparent that scenting conditions vary a good deal, enabling a bird dog on one day to wind birds and, almost at a trot, move fifty yards or more and point. The same dog on another day may run through and flush a covey without detecting them.

Because the human olfactory system is so limited in perceiving scent, it is impossible for us to test the factors directly responsible for the variations in scenting conditions. With bird hunting, the dog either finds his quarry or he does not, and the effect of scenting conditions is difficult to determine.

In contrast, the ability of hounds to follow a trail because of variations in scenting conditions can be readily quantitated. One day they run at top speed without even a temporary loss; the next they are able only to intermittently follow a trail slowly. One of the best books written on the subject, *The Mystery of Scent*, by Hugh B.C. Pollard, an Englishman, contains carefully compiled data concerning the ability of hounds to run a fox in varying weather conditions.

A number of years ago, I did a similar study while fox hunting at night, and I arrived at basically the same conclusions as Pollard. Pollard refined his data—using a combination of humidity, temperature, cloud cover, and wind (velocity and direction)—to develop a "scentometer" to quantitate scenting conditions. His fundamental postulate is that the hound's nose is actually sensing several different small hydrophilic substances (scent). These scent particles are attached to water vapor and disburse as the water evaporates. Scent must be highly specific for a given species. Whether or not there are specific scent particles for different sources of scent in the same animal is unknown: i.e., foot or body.

It follows that if relative humidity is near 100 percent, evaporation cannot occur. Thus, scenting conditions will be poor when rain is falling or in very heavy, early morning dew. Within a humidity range of 70 to 90 percent, a number of scent-containing particles evaporate and leave a trail. Conditions deteriorate with a lower humidity and fewer scent particles. Early morning (unless humidity is above 90 percent) and late afternoon usually provide the more optimal humidity ranges and, hence, better scenting conditions.

Wind is another noteworthy factor. Wind dispenses scent particles; therefore, they aren't concentrated in a small area near the ground. A light wind may actually help by enabling sufficient scent to occupy a larger area. On the other hand, a brisk wind disperses the particles too much and produces a deleterious effect. Clearly, if a significant wind is blowing, it is best to hunt the dogs in a direction against the wind. That way the scent is blown toward them and detected before they get too close to the birds and flush them. Many dogs, especially those with bird sense, hunt upwind instinctively or as a learned method.

Whether wind direction is important or not is moot: Voluminous folklore testifies to its effects, and statements such as "an east wind is not fit even to make a bargain, let alone for a dog to smell" are common. Humidity can be related to wind direction. Thus, the effect on scent ascribed to wind direction most likely is due to variations in humidity. Nevertheless, I have hunted with people who will not even go out if the wind is blowing from the northeast. Frankly, my experience says they are correct.

Temperature is important not only because of its effect on humidity but also because it has an effect on the "scentor," the dog. In hot weather, dogs often pant a great deal, which markedly impedes their ability to perceive scent. Another bit of folklore tells us that scent is best when the earth is warmer than the air. Maybe. My opinion is that diffusion of scent is affected very little by this factor.

In summary, the ideal conditions for scenting are no wind (or a south wind of less than 5 MPH), humidity between 80 and 90 percent, and a temperature between 40 and 60 degrees. The most adverse conditions are a northeast wind above 20 MPH, humidity of 100 percent or less than 60 percent, and temperature below freezing or higher than 80 degrees.

Even with all these data collected and analyzed, it seems to me that, at best, only about 25 percent of the mystery of scent can be revealed. Under the most adverse scenting conditions, I have seen pointers handle birds expertly; conversely, under "perfect" conditions, I have also seen them not able to smell at all. So much for scientific precision!

Odor from surrounding vegetation may also play a part. Scenting conditions in the upper South are generally marginal at best until a hard freeze is followed by a good rain, which kills the green vegetation and washes away all the odors emanating from the rotting residue. As a rule, scenting conditions are better after Christmas. In much of the lower South, however, freezing weather may not occur, and the dogs must contend with the odor of green vegetation throughout the hunting season.

I hunted recently in Florida, in an area where the wiregrass hadn't been burned for several years, and it had formed into a dense, matted layer on the ground. Even with otherwise favorable scenting conditions, the dogs couldn't trail or find dead or wounded birds in that cover, making it clear that the type and state of the vegetation frequented by the birds also has a major effect on scenting.

The concentration of scent and the areas covered by scent are of prime importance and related to the activity in which the birds are engaged. If the covey is huddled together under a bush, resting or hiding from predators, the scent is restricted to a small area; whereas, if the birds are moving and feeding and thus scattered, the scent is widely dispersed.

I have often heard that wild quail "hold their scent," especially after being flushed. At face value the notion seems like rubbish, but a lot of experienced hunters believe it. Numerous quail-hunting sages suggest that when hunting singles, it makes sense to give the birds a few minutes to redevelop their scent, after having been "air washed" during flight. Frankly, I abandoned this seemingly reasonable approach several years ago. Most of the birds I hunt don't sit still after landing; they race to the nearest swamp.

The final and most obvious factor in an understanding of scenting conditions is the acuity of the dog's smelling apparatus. It can vary greatly. Currently, I am blessed with Faith, a dog whose nose is vastly superior to those of her colleagues. Time and again she outperforms them when scenting conditions are marginal. I am convinced that a "good nose" is the prime factor in characterizing a superb bird dog.

Since early morning and late afternoon provide the best scenting conditions—in addition to the fact that these are the times the birds are moving—a true "meat" dog expends maximum effort during these periods. Often I've become exasperated, watching outstanding pointers only pretend to hunt until late in the day. Then, when this witching hour begins, as if by magic, they perk up, change demeanor, and become genuine hunting machines. To my mind, besides being first-class actors, these dogs have perceived the change in scenting conditions and decided that the time had arrived to do some serious work!

To summarize, the quality of scenting conditions, the vegetation in the hunting venue, the activity of the birds, and the dog's ability to perceive scent are all factors that play major roles in whether birds will be located and pointed correctly. Numerous other unknowns in the equation might, if one is persistent, be discovered and solved. However, my guess is that if we knew everything about scent and always found birds, much of the excitement of bird hunting would disappear.

Why Hunt Birds with Pointers?

Chapter X

It should be apparent to rational people that the choice of an English pointer as a bird-hunting companion is asking for a plethora of problems. When not hunting, they are aloof, high-strung, and tend to get into trouble. Even while hunting, pointers want to be boss, continually trying to make the rules and direct the show. In a word, they do not care whether or not you are part of the proceedings. A constant high level of stress accompanies staying on top of the situation by trying to convince the dog to function as part of a team. Another negative feature: Male English pointers love to fight, which is the major reason I've come to prefer females, who also fight, but generally stop short of crippling one another.

Since all of the pointing dogs (German short-hair pointers, several varieties of setters, Brittanys, and, now, even pointing Labradors) are capable of finding and pointing birds, why put up with the negative characteristics of English pointers? If the only reason for hunting is to spend a relaxing time outdoors with an enjoyable canine companion, I recommend the use of a different breed.

Let's examine why a dedicated bird hunter would choose an English pointer. Pointers have just one interest in life—hunting! Pointers don't develop a close bonding relationship; they don't make good pets. Also, they aren't likely to win "best of show" in bench competitions. With many other breeds, which function nicely as family companions or possibly bench-show champions, breeding to maintain superior hunting capabilities may play second fiddle. One needs only to look at the complete destruction of the Irish setter as a hunting dog, caused by selective breeding aimed at winning bench shows.

On the other hand, the single-mindedness of English pointers, I believe, is responsible for making them superior bird dogs. It makes no sense to own English pointers unless you hunt them. Over the years, this characteristic has led to keeping and breeding only the best hunters. Thus, the odds of obtaining a bird dog with a well-honed hunting heritage are considerably better with the English pointer.

A few other reasons for the choice: Pointers tolerate hot weather better than most breeds and are better adapted to the wide-ranging hunting necessary in much of the lower South. Also, anyone owning a longhaired dog must spend at least an hour after each hunt removing cockleburs from the coat.

Still, the positives listed are not likely to equal or cancel out the inevitable aggravation encountered when dealing with this breed, so we are back to square one: Why choose an English pointer when plenty of other breeds are touted as readily adaptable to bird hunting?

I've asked this question many times, often when trying to control a headstrong young pointer running out of control in the next county. I haven't really found an answer. Probably my choice is based on early experiences, which might mean that I am too contrary or stupid to adapt to anything new. This may well be the case, but I prefer to look elsewhere for the reason.

I've had the opportunity over the years to bird-hunt with reasonably competent examples of the other pointing breeds: English setters (I've owned several. My best, Pepper, I hunted with for nearly eight years); Irish setters; German short-hair pointers (bred recently, it seems, to mimic the characteristics of the English pointer); and big and medium-size Brittanys.

Although I've witnessed acceptable bird work from all of these breeds, they simply don't measure up in class, style, or whatever words are used to describe the picturesque scene of a pair of pointers covering a fifty-acre field with consummate speed, efficiency, and grace . . . before then slamming on the brakes to a stylish point. This scene never ceases to impress me.

So, why the English pointer? To put it in simple Uncle Remus terms, the other pointing breeds "Jes ain't right!"

Four 15-inch male beagles. They competed successfully in two-couple-pack field trials and excelled when rabbit hunting. Their "voices" ranged from Colonel's high-pitched squeal to Sport's mournful bawl. The chop-mouth tones from Sam and Duffy rounded out the quartet. Atlanta, Georgia, 1948.

Spot pointing a covey near my home in Atlanta—currently a major shopping center—1951.

Spot posing with a bird in his mouth. The deep cut on the right shoulder was caused by barbed wire. Thomasville, Georgia, 1953.

Spot and Don rode many miles in this dog trailer. The shotgun, a 20-gauge Parker, was the author's first bird gun. Cochran, Georgia, 1955.

The author's dressin' technique changed from "picker" to "skinner." This "pile of birds" was shot near Hawkinsville, Georgia, 1955.

Belle, though not stylish or pretty to look at, was a bird-finding machine. Here she's pointing near Albany, Georgia, 1960.

Spot still pointing at age thirteen. Bleckley County, Georgia, 1961.

Mack, lost for about two hours, was found on point. Bleckley County, Georgia, 1963.

Six foxhounds (Walker and July) that could really move a fox. When in full cry on a frosty night, their "music" surpassed the best symphony. With Minnie, Smokey, Frosty, Irene, Molly, and Beulah after him, "Brer Fox" had better skedaddle. Durham, North Carolina, 1964.

Rena, a nine-week-old puppy, pointing a bird wing. Durham, North Carolina, 1971.

Cricket pointing a quail, which is sitting under the limb in front of her in lower left corner of the picture. Orange County, North Carolina, 1972.

Rena's tail had to be docked about three inches because of continual trauma during hunting. She was an all-round superb bird dog. Orange County, North Carolina, 1974.

While hunting and pointing, Sandy carried her tail quite low. Although intense, she would not "come up to snuff" as a stylish bird dog. Orange County, North Carolina, 1975.

Gypsy pointing in Orange County, North Carolina, 1978.

Tiny showing off. Near Yee Haw Junction, Florida, 1983.

Pepper pointing. Near Yee Haw Junction, Florida, 1984.

Pepper and Tiny backing Hannah. Near Asheboro, North Carolina, 1986.

Hannah pointing a rare woods covey. Orange County, North Carolina,1986.

Hank on a stylish point. LaBelle, Florida, 1989.

Anne pointing and Lib II (far left) backing. Indiantown, Florida, 1991.

Lib II is pointing with a bird in her mouth; Joey looks impressed. Indiantown, Florida, 1993.

Sugar is backing in the foreground, and Hannah is pointing approximately seventy yards in front of her. Tabletop Butte can be seen in the background. Farson, Wyoming, 1995.

Missy's litter, age six weeks. Even at that young age, they were very, very impressive. Near Durham, North Carolina, 1996.

Seven pointers: one pointing and the rest backing. The entire contingent had been turned loose to be loaded into the swamp buggy for the morning hunt. When a single was discovered, they froze. Near Hobe Sound, Florida, 1996.

The author carrying a sage grouse while Faith points another. Farson, Wyoming, 1997.

Luke bringing home the "chicken." Farson, Wyoming, 1997.

Cody pointing sage grouse; note the spectacular scenery. Near Farson, Wyoming, 1997.

This is the "chain gang" waiting to be fed. Near Sitzmann's Motel in Farson, Wyoming, 1998.

The swamp buggy loaded with all sorts of paraphernalia ready for a day's hunt. Joey is adjusting the beeper collar on Cody. Hobe Sound, Florida, 1998.

Horatio (son) and Missy (mother) pointing. Indiantown, Florida, 1999.

Hamlet, age three, ponders: "To have them or not to have them—that is the question." Indiantown, Florida, 1999.

Joey and Cody examine the result of a broken axle in the new swamp buggy. No! It won't function as a three wheeler. Indiantown, Florida, 2001.

Luke, the Younger, pointing with unusual intensity. Indiantown, Florida, 2003.

As with most pictures of pointing dogs taken in the field, only the "rear-end" features can be seen, as Horatio and Faith demonstrate. Near Bassinger, Florida, 2002.

Jeb showing off. Indiantown, Florida, 2004.

Scylla pointing a bird wing at age eight weeks. Orange County, North Carolina, 2004.

Faith, age fourteen—still the "gold standard." Orange County, North Carolina, 2004.

Ulysses, age nine months, and Mama Lou on point. Indiantown, Florida, 2005.

Horatio and Humphrey have twenty years of experience—the birds don't have a chance. Indiantown, Florida, 2006.

Tyre shows real style. Indiantown, Florida, 2007.

The author, mesmerized by Jeb and Scylla on point, the essence of quail hunting. Indiantown, Florida, 2007.

Bard showing off. He's learned a lot about Florida quail. Indiantown, Florida, 2007.

Virgo finally realizes, "I think I've got it: Point, not pounce." Indiantown, Florida, 2008.

Pepper and Tyre pointing a split covey. Indiantown, Florida, 2007.

Training Pointers

Chapter XI

"The trainer must have more sense than the dog" should be the first maxim in any bird dog training manual. Given the relative IQ levels between humans and canines, there would seem at first blush to be no problem . . . not necessarily so. In the context of training, the word "sense" assumes a meaning specifically related to the human's ability to develop and control the skills of a bird dog. I've known many extremely smart people who were utter failures as bird dog mentors.

I'm reminded of a time years ago watching a mule "snake" logs. The driver struggled in vain to force the mule to move the logs in a designated manner.

"What's the problem?" I asked the sawmill owner who was shaking his head, clearly disgusted.

"The mule has a lot more sense than the driver," he explained. "It'll take the mule a couple months to get him trained."

If your bird-dog pupil has similar characteristics, give up; this dog is too smart for you to instruct successfully.

The information that follows, gleaned over many years, will at the least, I hope, prevent the reader from ruining a good prospect. There are scores of books, articles, pamphlets, and, now, videotapes that describe methods "guaranteed" to produce an outstanding bird dog. Generally, they are based on the assumption that all pointing dogs behave the same. First premise: Eschew advice from any "expert" who touts a method that can be used with equal success on Brittanys and English pointers.

When training other pointing breeds, I offer the same advice I gave a colleague years ago when he asked for help developing an Irish setter: "Make the dog a pet or give it away—then get yourself a pointer."

Assuming that training English pointers is the job at hand, first define the ultimate goal of the training process. In my case, I use a vehicle to cover a large acreage containing widely scattered coveys of quail. To be effective in these circumstances, a trained pointer must hunt a wide pattern in the direction the vehicle is moving, intelligently seeking and hunting the birdy places. At other times, when walking after singles, the dog should hunt fairly close to the cover I designate—not a half-mile away.

If a bird is inadvertently flushed, the dog must stop. When trailing, the dog should move toward the birds as fast as feasible, and not potter. If the covey is running, the dog must know how to follow closely without flushing. It goes without saying that the dog must be steady on point and back willingly, which means backing on sight without the need of either verbal or electronic correction. The point should be intense without flagging, but not strained. I don't insist on either a perpendicular tail or a high head, and I don't mind if the dog moves when I fire. After the flush, the dog must remain in the vicinity to retrieve (assuming I've killed something, which frequently isn't the case). Where retrieving is concerned, my only requirement is that the dog find the downed birds without an undue amount of cajoling and bring them to me in a relatively unmacerated state. Acceptable retrieving assumes a willingness to chase cripples.

The single most important aspect of training is the selection of the trainee. If the genetic makeup is excellent, it's difficult, though not impossible, to ruin the dog. If given the proper opportunity, most pointers accomplish 90 percent of the training themselves.

How do you select a good prospect? When possible, choose a dog between eight and twelve months old. By this age it is easier to determine the important qualities: intelligence, desire and ability to hunt, and acuity of the nose. The latter is by far the most important. In fact, at least in my experience, lacking superior scenting ability will relegate the prospect to mediocrity.

If the choice is made at six to eight weeks of age, which usually happens, then the hunting qualities of the parents must be relied upon entirely. Personally, I like to see both parents in the field. Don't forget: The bitch is at least as important as the stud in imparting desired traits. A high-powered stud dog bred to a typical brood bitch (a female who flunked out as a hunter) isn't apt to produce first-rate hunting puppies.

If available, the quality of dogs from a previous litter by the same sire and dam can be examined. Studying the pedigree that documents the field trial exploits of the puppy's family can be helpful but is not a substitute for firsthand knowledge of the hunting qualities of the sire and dam. Regarding the sex, I prefer females. Generally they're easier to train and not as likely to fight. Many hunters whose opinions I respect disagree with me.

Once the puppy is brought home, don't you, or anyone in your family, fall in love with it, at least not until the training is far enough along so it is relatively certain the dog will become a "keeper." Little is more heartbreaking than culling a worthless dog that has nuzzled itself into your heart. The hard truth is that failure to cull mediocre performers is the single largest impediment to owning class bird dogs.

What's the best age for a dog to begin training? There are two extremes: 1) Start yard training when he's weaned, then five or six months later train with birds and hope to have a finished product when the dog is one year old; 2) let the puppy run unrestrained and have a good time for a year, then begin training. Proponents of the former technique claim that early instruction encourages the desire to hunt with the trainer, and the dog isn't allowed to develop bad habits. Advocates of the second approach feel that by correcting the puppy too early in life may compromise the hunting drive and style. I tend to advocate this latter approach, with a few modifications.

I begin yard-breaking a dog when it's about six months old. This includes teaching the puppy its name, to come when called, and to stop on hearing "Whoa!" Regarding the name, it doesn't seem to matter. My dogs really only respond to "son-of-a-bitch." Also, at this time, I begin to teach the dog to retrieve. One trainer I know swears that force-breaking dogs to retrieve ranks first among the things needed to be done early. However, this man's livelihood depends on force-breaking dogs to retrieve; thus, he may not be entirely objective. It is probably a good idea to shoot over the puppy while he's eating (using a .22 blank pistol), though none of mine have had problems with gun-shyness.

If selected properly, the dog will be bold, aggressive, and reasonably tractable. It is essential to determine quickly the mixture of reward and punishment needed to persuade the dog to complete the task at hand. Reward and punishment are the keys; their use must be tailored to the individual dog. A technique heavy on punishment that works with one dog will quickly ruin another. In my experience, much more is accomplished by praising the dog for correct behavior than punishing it for malfeasance. I believe significant punishment is only appropriate when the dog clearly understands what he is supposed to do but consistently refuses to comply.

When the dog is yard-trained, it's time to hunt. He will progress faster if he has had time to run loose, exercise, and develop hunting skills and stamina. Now what he needs most is exposure to quail—a task best accomplished with pen-raised birds. This gives him the chance to run up birds, chase them, and basically just have a good time.

After you're convinced the dog is birdy, the natural pointing instinct can be exploited. Most dogs, at the least, will flash point, and the task is to extend the time until you're willing for him to break point. If the dog has been properly "Whoa!" broke, this won't be a problem. (By "Whoa!" broke, I mean stop on command in the field, even when the dog's mind is on something besides listening to you.)

It's good to praise the dog while he's pointing, and gently rubbing his back will help him hold his point. Care should be taken not to break the dog's concentration with too much attention or you may cause flagging to develop. Once you can rely upon the dog to be steady, it is time to start shooting the flushed birds.

A problem with released birds is they frequently walk around in front of the dog, refusing to fly. When this occurs, keep the dog pointed while you kick up the birds. At this juncture, the dog should not be allowed to catch birds, either in the air or on the ground.

If a dog learns to catch birds, much of the effort expended to make him steady will be lost, and it could take several months to correct the problem. If, after considerable effort, the dog remains headstrong and continues to run up and chase the birds, the best approach is to bring him to where the misadventures occurred, give him hell, and make him point until released.

The amount of hell will depend upon your prior assessment of what is needed to gain his undivided attention. Obviously, repeated bad behavior will ruffle your composure, but if you lose your temper, quit for the day. Working with a dog when you're angry is a losing proposition. (I wish I could always adhere to my own advice on this subject.) On the bright side, learning to stay calm under bird-dog-induced stress is helpful to your cardiovascular system.

Once the dog remains pointed until you flush and shoot, he is ready to be hunted. Then, first of all, make sure he hunts with you and not by himself. I've found this is best accomplished with a shock collar on low power, demonstrated to the dog before reaching the field. I have found the optimal way to introduce the shock collar is with an antibark collar, employed around the age of six months. Shock collars are very helpful in making the dog hunt with you, but using them to correct errors in handling quail during an early stage of training may make the puppy bird shy.

Running the newcomer with a well-trained older dog that is willing to put up with puppy misadventures may accelerate the process, especially in learning where to find birds. The down side is that the pupil may rely entirely on the teacher and depend too much on him. If the young dog does not run independently most of the time, hunt him by himself. When the older dog is used, backing skills can be readily taught.

When the hunting stage of training begins, two things will determine the young dog's future development: The amount of time spent hunting in a territory containing quail and how consistently the trainer behaves. During the training period, forget about killing birds. Shoot only when the situation is ideal. Don't shoot at singles that have been inadvertently flushed, but only at pointed birds. Before shooting, always demand that the dog point, that the other dog back, and if a bird is killed or wounded, it must be retrieved.

And always, to reiterate, be consistent. Letting a dog misbehave without correction several times in a row, then losing your temper and overcorrecting, is a guaranteed prescription for failure. Once you establish that you are in charge and will not tolerate improper performance (and the dog understands this fact), you're well on the way to developing a trained pointer. Regardless of when serious training begins, it's important to avoid situations that later on may result in bizarre or unwarranted behavior. Nip in the bud any bad habits, and stay away from significant traumatic experiences.

As a general rule, the hunting instinct of the young pointers may be encouraged if allowed to run loose and develop on their own, but for every rule there is an exception. Several years ago I was given a fifteen month-old, well-bred pointer female with little formal training that had been allowed to run loose. When I began working with her, she hunted hard but wasted a lot of time looking up into trees. She did OK hunting quail, but searching trees remained her primary focus. I mentioned this habit to her former owner. After thinking a minute he said, "During the early months of her life, she ran loose near a barn populated with pigeons. She spent the better part of each day chasing them from the barn, to the trees, to the pasture, and back again." That solved the mystery, but the habit had become so ingrained that I disposed of her to an unsuspecting Yankee who didn't know whether quail were ground or tree birds!

Frequently, a young dog that runs loose will become an ardent rabbit chaser. This problem by itself is not difficult to remedy, but the dogs may learn to hunt primarily in swamps rather than in quail habitat.

Far more harmful to the dog can be a single traumatic experience, which results in a lifelong behavior pattern that may prove impossible to correct. The oft-employed technique of testing gun-shyness by firing a 12-gauge shotgun directly over a young puppy's head has ruined many potentially fine gun dogs.

I nearly rendered useless an incessantly barking puppy, Bonnie, with one of the early model bark suppressor collars. Once I had buckled it in place, she started barking, as expected, and the collar did its duty, shocking her. However, the collar continued shocking until I managed to wrestle it off. All Bonnie took away from this experience was an everlasting fear of training collars. She even refused to hunt with one around her neck. Fortunately, she required little correction in the field and developed into an acceptable bird dog.

Several years ago, I acquired a three-year-old female pointer that, although not particularly stylish, ranked as an outstanding bird dog, except for one quirk. She wouldn't hunt in the proximity of cows—proximity defined by her as about a half mile. I have never had much luck finding birds in cow pastures, but most of the areas I hunted in North Carolina required such crossings. When I would start on the trek, Sandy would refuse to follow. Usually she'd go back to the truck and pout or, if she knew the terrain, make a wide detour around the pasture, wasting a half hour or more. It turned out that Sandy, at age three months, had been stepped on by a cow. Though not seriously hurt, she had been so frightened that she refused to return to the barn where she had been raised.

The practice (not so much today, but in the past) of allowing young dogs to run loose on a farm meant introducing them to a variety of domestic critters. Since deleting Sunday's dinner did not ingratiate them with the lady of the house, they had to be taught not to kill chickens, often a difficult concept to instill. An often-used method of obviating the problem involved confining the puppy with a mean rooster that proceeded to kick and spur the hell out of the young dog, thereby convincing it that chickens were better left alone. Not infrequently it worked too well; the puppy learned to run from all fowl, including quail . . . not an ideal trait for a bird dog. Young dogs are extremely impressionable and must be protected from traumatic experiences.

Fairly early in the training process, a trainer must decide how much time and effort he is willing to expend on a specific dog before throwing in the towel. Remember, only very few pointers come into the world as finished bird dogs. Once yard training begins, it won't take long to discover how tractable the dog is and how rapidly he learns. Similarly, once actual work with birds is begun, the dog's prowess quickly becomes manifest in key areas—amount of bottom, style, desire to hunt, and general level of intelligence. My own rule of thumb: Unless the dog is truly worthless, give the effort one season.

The shock collar has been a boon to bird dog trainers, but if used excessively it can produce: 1) a bird-shy dog, 2) an unruly dog (unless the collar is always worn), and 3) when the collar is worn, a timid and restrained hunter. The primary need for a shock collar is to keep the dog from running off (bolting) and to hunt in an acceptable pattern.

In the past, numerous methods were used to stop bolting. The worst was shooting the dog in the rear with #8 shot, and while occasionally effective, this method was not infrequently fatal. Another discarded method of controlling the dog's range involved having him hunt, dragging a heavy chain attached to his collar, but this often severely traumatized the front legs. Appropriate use of the shock collar has rendered these other approaches totally unnecessary.

The other major use of the shock collar is to break the dog from running deer, killing armadillos, chasing pigs, and hunting any variety of other creatures. The degree of shock depends on the dog, but I've found a warning buzzer that alerts the dog that a significant shock is coming if his behavior isn't corrected is the best approach. Personally, I do not advise its use to correct errors in handling quail since the dog could be rendered bird shy.

The recent introduction of a beeper locator has helped training immeasurably. When I think back over fifty-odd years and thousands of hours wasted searching for lost dogs (many of them pointed just a few hundred yards away from me), I realize that the beeper collar is a major advance. I'm no longer comfortable hunting without it. For some reason, the beep doesn't seem to disturb either bird dog or quail.

When is the dog finished with its training? Basically, bird dogs are never completely trained. Each hunting trip should aim for the dogs to function as closely to perfection as possible. Striving for such a goal makes the hunting far more exciting and memorable than merely shooting a few quail.

Rather than expend the effort yourself, you can pay a professional trainer to do the job. Problem is, as good trainers become known, they often accept more dogs than they can possibly handle, and results deteriorate. Don't expect any trainer to deliver a dog with hunting experience or "bird sense." A finished dog today is defined as one who will point, back, and retrieve.

A pitfall to avoid is pouring too much money into a puppy that doesn't develop well. Most professional trainers will continue to work with the dog, running up large bills on what likely will be a mediocre performer. Anyone hiring a trainer should frequently evaluate the dog's progress. At $300 or more per month, it's easy to spend a lot of money and come away with nothing. In my opinion, a professional trainer may be best employed if the efforts are confined to a single task, such as force-breaking to retrieve.

Frequently, the hunter becomes convinced during the first year that he has a well-trained dog. The next year most often is spent in frustration—a humbling experience. I'm not sure why, but pointers during their second hunting season (the terrible twos) take delight in trying your patience. When you know the dog knows what to do and nonetheless screws up, not losing your temper is almost impossible. Don't despair. There's good news. The dog not only will return to form the next year but likely will be better.

Like any athlete, a bird dog is very competitive. Some perform well when hunting alone but become too aggressive when hunted with a strange dog. Failure to back is most often the problem, and can be exasperating. However, if the other dog is guilty of frequent false pointing or flagging significantly while on point, the failure to back may not be entirely your dog's fault.

Dogs have good and bad days for a number of reasons. They may be sick, scenting conditions might be poor, they may not be in top shape, you may have hunted them too hard, exhaust fumes may have thrown them off stride, it's too hot, or they have sand spurs in their feet. The list is much longer. Also, after several hours of hunting and finding nothing, dogs become disinterested. It's aggravating to hunt all day, find only one covey, and then have the dog flush the birds, but it is all part of the game.

After considering the many hassles involved in raising and training a puppy, many might ask: Why not buy a well-trained dog that is ready to hunt? It is easier said than done. Personally, I do not derive significant pleasure wrestling with the learning curve of puppies, and would prefer spending my time enjoying the exploits of trained dogs. Thus, I've expended considerable effort locating and buying trained bird dogs, often with disastrous and expensive results. By trained, I mean I expect the dog to perform up to the standards described above. At present, the main difficulty is the extraordinary cost incurred obtaining such a dog (made much worse if the seller finds out you're a doctor).

A reasonably good bird dog fifty years ago cost no more than $100. That meant, and I am not joking, the trainer received, at best, five cents for every hour working with the dog. No one today is willing to toil for such a wage. Thus, the current price of $2,500 to $3,500 is actually more in line with the effort expended in developing a quality bird dog. (In this respect, I must recognize Mr. Jarrett Thompson from Rosanky, Texas. In the past several years, I have gotten several outstanding pointers from him, and, although not cheap, they have always performed as represented.)

The truth is, though, one can spend a lot of money and still not get a good hunting dog. In fact, the only sure-fire way to obtain an outstanding dog cheaply is to bamboozle a widow who doesn't realize the value of her deceased husband's dog—unfortunately, an infrequent opportunity.

It's essential to test the dog, if possible, in your own hunting venue. Two or three hours should be sufficient for a knowledgeable hunter to determine whether the dog is acceptable. You won't learn much about the dog in this time period but probably enough to make an informed choice.

I have been on both sides of the issue regarding the appropriate length of a trial. A supposed buyer kept one of my dogs for two weeks, brought him back hunted to exhaustion and said, "I really don't need the dog this year, but I might try him again next."

Luckily for both of us, this worthy hurried off before I could find a heavy object. The point is, though, I recognize the problems facing a dealer when someone requests an extensive trial.

The situation is more amenable to solution if the prospective dog is located within reasonable driving distance. If not, the cost of shipping can quickly mount up, and the dog might not survive the experience. It's happened to me twice: A dog I shipped by freight got crushed by other baggage, and one of my best dogs was carelessly allowed to sit at an airport in subzero weather and contracted pneumonia. Airlines have cleaned up their acts in recent years in this regard, and I have had no more problems. I never forgave the one, however, that left my dog in the cold.

Years ago, a well-known dealer in Oklahoma once offered to trade a trained dog to me for a gun and cash. We agreed, sight unseen, that the dog was worth $500 and the gun, $300. I sent him the gun and a postdated check for $200, and he shipped the dog to me for a ten-day trial. Everything seemed in order until I saw the dog. He wandered out of the shipping crate, and though he might once have seen a pointer, a pointer he was not. I stared at a nondescript hound that had no notion of what a bird dog was supposed to do.

I contacted the dealer, stopped payment on the check, and shipped the dog back. Then, I waited for my gun to be returned . . . and waited . . . and waited. I am still waiting! It finally dawned on me that the man had developed an ingenious method of stealing guns. Since I had paid the cost of shipping, his investment amounted to zero, plus he got his dog back to cheat someone else. My lawyer told me to forget about suing the crook since he lived in another state.

One point to remember is the fact that a dog that has excelled in field trials may not be competent in a hunting venue. Success in open trials indicates the dog is energetic and wide-ranging, but, if really talented, he will not be available at any price. If unsuccessful, he's likely to be a bolting idiot. If trained for trials designed to simulate bird hunting, the dog may be skilled at pointing, backing, and steady to wing and shot. He will not have the experiences with wild quail that makes an outstanding hunter. In fact, the only thing outstanding will be the asking price.

A final matter of note: Remember, sooner or later, unless the dog meets an untimely death, he'll begin to backslide and, like an old man, grow senile. Especially when a pointer has been a top dog, he won't, because of his competitiveness, adjust well to the slowing-down process. Usually, wide-ranging dogs do not shorten the length of their pattern, but run at a much slower pace, often unable to keep up. The problem is highlighted when they are hunting with younger dogs that find the birds first, relegating the proud old dogs to the unworthy position of permanent backer.

Sadly, the older dog frequently attempts to attract attention by reverting to untrained behavior, such as failing to back, flushing birds, chasing pigs, and killing armadillos. I find this aspect of dealing with pointers very difficult, i.e., a dog you've depended on for five or six years suddenly behaves like an untrained idiot. Such malfeasance will test your patience and break your heart. To avoid this loss of dignity, I hunt an older dog alone or with a started puppy, so the senior can still be "top dog."

I try to remain philosophical and hope someone will help me when I get lost in my dotage.

Convincing a Pointer to Retrieve

Chapter XII

Dedicated bird hunters share the belief that the day isn't complete until all birds, either killed or wounded, have been recovered. If necessary, they will spend considerable time searching through matted grass, honeysuckle tangles, and briars, even digging in gopher holes to assure this conclusion. The best and most efficient way to collect downed quarry, however, is with a dog dedicated to retrieving. Therein lies the problem. English pointers, as a rule, are not reliable natural retrievers.

One of the proudest moments in a bird-hunter's day occurs after a covey rise and successful shot when he proudly announces, "Dead bird." Most pointers, at least mine, respond with a "Who-gives-a-damn?" look. Pointers are not instinctively driven to retrieve; it's no fun for them. Retrieving subtracts from the time they could spend hunting and pointing another covey.

In order for a pointer to retrieve reliably, he should be force-broken. Force-broken implies that the dog will retrieve, like it or not. Force-breaking to retrieve requires patience and consistency but is relatively easy to achieve if you commit the time. Better yet, it is something that can be accomplished in the off-season.

Of the two components to retrieving, the most important by far—infrequently dealt with by gun-dog mavens—is for the dog to locate the dead or wounded bird. The next is to transport the bird to the hunter without partially or wholly digesting it. Thus, the chief hurdle to overcome is the pointer's reluctance to look for downed birds.

When searching for dead birds, the typical pointer will run around at top speed, head held high in the air (as if actually trying to avoid finding the bird). If by chance he finds it, all well and good; if not, he's ever alert to run away and start hunting again. Only if the hunter is persistent, making it clear that hunting will not be resumed until the bird is found, will a pointer really work on the objective.

This is the attitude of pointers force-broken to retrieve, and without such training, retrieving is nonexistent.

Recently, I witnessed a vivid example of this attitude. I winged a bird that fell in thick grass, then watched Hannah pretend to look for it, interspersing her "effort" with frequent episodes of running off to begin hunting again. When I refused to follow her, she'd return and pout. After ten minutes of this nonsense, she decided I was serious. Hannah put her nose to the ground and quickly found the bird, bringing it to me with a disgusted "Can-we-get-down to-business-now?" look.

If it is tough with a seasoned pro like Hannah, how can a young pointer be persuaded to hunt dead birds? My advice is not to shout "Dead bird" unless you are sure, and be consistent and persistent. Never let the dog begin hunting again until the bird is properly retrieved. Stay in the area all day, if necessary. Luckily, most pointers will demonstrate enthusiasm for running down and catching wounded birds once they have identified that the bird is alive.

I've owned two pointers that liked to retrieve, and each developed the skill for the same reason. When young, they were hunted with experienced "covey dogs" and spent much of their time backing. As far as I can determine, backing is something a pointer will avoid unless assured that refusal to back will bring swift retribution. Both these dogs learned, however, that when the covey flew and dead birds lay on the ground, the other dogs weren't interested in retrieving. They accepted the retrieving role, I believe, because it allowed them "to shine." When these dogs grew older and able to find birds by themselves, their interest in retrieving waned.

The second component of retrieving, delivering the bird in an unmacerated state, is a necessary attribute of every finished bird dog. Many dogs have the irritating habit of picking up the bird and running around in a circle, out of reach, ultimately dropping it under a bush when you're not looking. As far as retrieving goes, I'm not a perfectionist who demands that birds be placed in my pocket, or carried only by the head, but I do insist that the quail be brought to my vicinity, rather than dropped haphazardly ten yards away.

A hard-mouthed dog may deliver a bird in conditions varying from a light tooth mark on the breast to a bloody mass of flesh and feathers. If it is badly shot up, the dog is more likely to engulf the remains. Of course, it is best if the dog never begins to chew the birds. My best retriever, Tiny, began her career as a tender-mouthed dog, but after several wounded birds escaped, she "solved" the problem with a through-and-through bite. Administering this coup de grace became part of her retrieving procedure.

Hannah developed an interesting approach to delivering wounded birds. She'd bring the bird to a spot just out of my reach, spit it out, and gleefully watch it run off. She absolutely refused further involvement, indicating with a derisive look, "If you'd kill, instead of wound, there would be no problem."

A number of approaches have been suggested to break a dog from being hard-mouthed, including having him retrieve birds laced with pepper or festooned with various sharp objects. However, using these types of punishment will likely break the dog from retrieving entirely.

Havilah Babcock, in *Jaybirds Go to Hell on Friday*, described a technique to break a hard-mouthed dog by stuffing several birds down his throat until he became violently ill. This approach may work, but the application seems disgusting. With the scarcity of quail these days, it isn't a particularly useful method.

Despite the general reluctance of pointers to retrieve, several exceptions to the rule stand out in my mind. I saw a wounded bird fall into a fairly fast-flowing stream between a log and the opposite overhanging bank. Rena jumped in, swam to the log, smelled the bird, but couldn't locate it. She swam to shore, studied the situation, then paddled back to the log. She ducked her head under the water, came up on the other side of the log, grabbed the bird and ferried it back. A most impressive feat, I thought.

Bubba trailed a wounded bird to a gopher hole, and I saw him spend fifteen minutes enlarging the hole. The opening he dug in the soft, sandy Florida soil became so large he disappeared into it, with only the tip of his tail showing. Finally, he emerged, holding the bird firmly in his mouth. Hunting with such a peerless retriever can puff up one's ego. However, there's a reasonable chance the hole also contains a rattlesnake, so it's wise to restrain your dog from such excavations.

Finally, one may be treated to seeing a bird dog with a dead bird in its mouth pointing another bird. In wild-bird hunting, this situation occurs infrequently, unless single birds are close together. However, in preserve quail hunting it can be a reasonably common occurrence. It's an impressive sight and raises the question of how a bird dog can smell a live bird while holding a dead bird directly under its nose. I have no idea. On the other hand, most of my bird dogs refuse to hunt until they have covered their entire bodies with the most foul-smelling material available, and in spite of this overpowering odor, they seem to have no trouble in finding quail.

In summary, pointers are haphazard retrievers. If you want the job done well, get a Labrador.

What Can You Do with a Pointer in September?

Chapter XIII

My upland bird hunting experiences until 1988 were limited primarily to hunting *Colinus virginianus* (bobwhite quail). In fact, in pursuit of this endeavor, I had walked or ridden over much of the Southeast, including southern Virginia, the Carolinas, Alabama, Georgia, Florida, and frankly, I had no desire to expand my horizons to include other game.

Joey had been persuaded by his brother-in-law, a big-game guide in Wyoming, to help him during the busy antelope, mule deer, and elk seasons. Since the antelope season opened first, they spent the first three weeks in the sage-covered desert north of Farson, Wyoming. In this locale Joey found "sage chickens" (sage grouse) as well as several other species of grouse in the nearby mountains. He'd taken three of our pointers along to determine whether they could handle something other than quail.

The airplane trip (from West Palm Beach to Rock Springs, Wyoming) proved uneventful, except for Joey's momentary concern that Hannah might be turned away by the airport metal detector. She had been peppered on two occasions with birdshot by clients who apparently couldn't distinguish between a bird and a bird dog. Fortunately, they let her on board, the metal detector apparently not adept at picking up #8 birdshot.

When I saw Joey at the start of quail season in south Florida, he described hunting sage grouse as a "real hoot." Hannah, in particular, had stood out. Joey identified two problems, the first of which was trying to keep the dog within two or three miles of the hunter. Secondly, there was the tendency for the grouse to "spook" (flush out of range while the dogs were pointing). One of the three pointers never overcame the first problem; he stayed lost for most of the trip. By the end of the season, however, the other two dogs had learned to handle sage grouse reasonably well. Joey assured me that I would thoroughly enjoy this new bird-hunting experience, and he convinced me to join him the next year. (I'm not sure how he does it, but Joey can talk me into anything.)

At any rate, when the first week of September rolled around, I stowed myself and my bird hunting gear aboard an airplane and flew to Rock Springs, Wyoming, to begin the new adventure. Joey had driven out with the dogs—six of them this time—ten days earlier, so that they would be acclimated and ready to hunt. The hunting truck had been equipped with a dog box and a seat on top, so I was able to see the dogs. It was similar to the rig I used in Florida.

My plane arrived about noon, and we traveled the sixty miles from Rock Springs to Farson (population 325) in the hunting truck. The landscape was breathtaking with several million acres of rolling dry land covered variably with sage, sand, a sprinkling of antelope, an occasional tuft of grass and an enormous number of jack rabbits.

We hunted near the Continental Divide, that ridge of the Rockies that separates streams that become rivers flowing either toward the Atlantic or the Pacific oceans. I could see the Wind River Mountain Range and so much more—simply a spectacular view. Even more impressive was the fact that we were the only bird hunters in evidence.

I learned later that the standard method the local citizens used to hunt sage grouse involved driving along a road early in the morning or late in the evening, especially near alfalfa fields, hoping to spot a bird. If these hunters used a dog, it was one of the fuzzy hunting breeds generally used for retrieving. True, such foraging might quickly stock one's freezer, but I can't honestly classify it as bird hunting. That our approach stood in radical variance with local custom was emphasized every time we met other hunters, most of whom had never seen a pointer bird dog nor had any idea what such a creature did.

We began hunting by driving along one of the seismographic access roads, and after a few minutes, I spied an apparition standing straight ahead. On close inspection, it appeared to be a bird slightly larger but with the same color and configuration of a Plymouth Rock hen.

"That's one of them," Joey shouted.

"Really," I exclaimed. "Are you sure it's not an escapee from a chicken farm?"

The bird launched itself, exhibiting all the grace of a barnyard chicken. Once in the air, it flew just above the sage and disappeared over a knoll. Turning out two of the dogs, we started hunting the area.

Sage grouse droppings an inch or so long were ubiquitous, covering the landscape in various concentrations. I found out later that if you don't find droppings, you don't find sage grouse, but the converse isn't true. Only when the droppings are green, indicating freshness, is it certain the birds are close-by.

I was struck by the pungent odor of the sage itself. It was so strong, in fact, that it seemed impossible our dogs could discriminate bird scent. I reasoned, though, that if they could roll around in foul-smelling, rancid refuse (their usual *modus operandi*) and still detect quail, perhaps they could overcome the sage odor as well.

This first trip to Wyoming, on Joey's advice, I dressed as I would have in the wintertime in Florida, but the temperature suddenly dropped below freezing, accompanied by sleet and a chilling, 30-MPH wind. I shivered in a short-sleeved shirt, although luckily, the blizzard came and went in an hour, and I felt just fine after thawing out.

Late in the evening, Hannah pointed, and I walked toward her. Approximately fifteen yards away, two ungainly creatures laboriously took to the air. The grouse flew directly away from me, and I fired twice. They kept going. The thought flashed in my head that Joey, as was his custom, had bought the least expensive shotgun shells available, perhaps even loaded without shot. Anyway, I had been awake twenty hours, had been jostled around in a truck on the desert, had even endured a blizzard, but missing those birds—what a letdown!

One of the sage grouse fell some five hundred yards from where it flushed, and the ever-alert Hannah found it. The majority of shot had stuck on the feathers without penetrating. Although almost impossible to miss, grouse are difficult to stop if hit low in the body, particularly with inexpensive, easily deformed shot. That evening, I purchased some high-brass, 12-gauge shells loaded with 1½ ounces of copper-plated #5 shot. From then on, killing grouse presented no problem.

In the two remaining days, we flushed a number of coveys and singles. For a Southern quail hunter, it was quite a different sight seeing fifteen or more three-to-four-pound birds struggle to get off the ground at the same time. Hannah, Lib II, and Anne took to the excitement and handled the birds effectively. Our other dogs hunted for quail, never figuring out the new program. I think they equated grouse with sandhill cranes or large water birds that frequent Florida—birds they had been taught to ignore.

The behavior of the birds varied. About 70 percent, usually the younger ones, did not flush wild. However, when they stood up and started looking over the sage, they were preparing to exit—either by flying or running (actually their gait is best described as waddling or trudging). After flushing, they usually flew in a straight line, but due to the rolling landscape it was hard to judge their flight precisely. Even when one landed, the sameness of the terrain made exact location virtually impossible.

The best part for me was having the dogs in evidence at all times, running a wide pattern three-quarters of a mile to either side and in front of the truck. In South Florida, wide-ranging dogs have a penchant for disappearing into palmetto thickets.

"Thanks, Joey," I said, when it came time to leave. "It's been a once-in-a-lifetime experience—two trips rolled into one: My first and my last." In other words, I would not be back.

"You'll come here again," he smiled.

"How do you know?" I didn't believe him.

"There ain't," he said, "anything else you can hunt with a pointer bird dog in September."

It turned out he was right. The next year about the middle of June, I grew restless and purchased the airline ticket.

From then on, every September I've made the same trip to Wyoming to hunt sage grouse. About two weeks before the season begins, the efficient Joey drives his truck and a trailer loaded with twelve to fifteen pointers (this kind of hunting is excellent for training and conditioning) and three or four mules (eagerly sought by big-game guides) to Wyoming. On the return trip, he brings alfalfa hay and the dogs back home.

Nights we reside in Sitzmann's Motel, where the always hardworking Mickey and her children prepare superb and bountiful meals in the nearby restaurant. We've met a number of hardy local citizens in the restaurant and have learned about raising sheep and living in cold, dry weather. Temperatures may reach thirty below zero in winter. Cold weather like this is hard for me to imagine; the water pipes have to be buried twelve to fifteen feet underground, compared to eighteen inches in Piedmont North Carolina.

A recent topic of discussion out there has been the continuing spirited battle between the ranchers and the government over the reintroduction of wolves. The ranchers claim, probably correctly, that this raises havoc with both sheep and wildlife.

The sage desert landscape is seemingly unaffected by the passage of time. The Oregon Trail ran close to Farson, and ruts made by wagon wheels, as the settlers moved west 150 years ago, are still visible.

On several occasions, I've had the opportunity to observe the fascinating sport of falconry. Falcons are used to hunt sage grouse during the fall and early winter (sage grouse season is extended for falconry). The participants use a pointing dog first to locate the grouse. Then the falcon is released and the bird flushed. To say the least, these hunters are a dedicated group. They must go afield several times each week in order to maintain the falcon in hunting condition. I was surprised to learn about a major problem they encounter: Falcons are especially vulnerable to predation by golden eagles.

The dogs have taken to sage-grouse hunting with various degrees of proficiency. Because the scenting conditions are often horrible (a combination of arid air, sage odor, and a constant high wind), a successful pointer needs an exceptionally good nose. But if the dog will stop and hold when a single bird gets inadvertently flushed, the remaining birds of the covey are frequently dispersed over a wide enough area so all of them don't become airborne, allowing the hunter to get within shooting range. Both stopping to flush and backing at a distance are essential features of a proficient sage-grouse dog.

Despite poor scenting conditions, I've witnessed some outstanding dog work in Wyoming. Faith's superior nose allowed her to perform way above her peers. In fact, her ability to locate and handle sage grouse is nothing short of spectacular. All of our top-notch dogs cover a wide range of land methodically, locating grouse with their brains, as well as their noses. Three or four days of continued hunting is hard on the dogs, especially their feet (a main reason we take so many along), because much of the land is covered with shale. Interestingly, though the landscape doesn't seem to vary, the grouse congregate in the same areas year after year. I suppose they know why they prefer given locations, but I have not been smart enough to figure it out. For some strange reason, we have by far the best luck from about 10:00 A.M. until noon—not early in the morning nor late in the evening as with most other upland game.

I have to admit what to do with grouse meat presents a problem. It's a dark red, foul-tasting (no pun intended) meat that a great chef might possibly be able to make barely palatable. That's if it's eaten just before the passing-out stage of drunkenness—otherwise, no.

Some say that younger grouse are a delicacy, but not for me. The taste ranges from awful to inedible. However, a fellow doctor who accompanied me on several hunts has the problem solved. Each year he takes grouse home and gives them to "friends" he thoroughly dislikes.

A major attraction of Wyoming sage-grouse hunting is the solitude and vast beauty of the place. (We avoid the beginning of antelope season, when a large number of hunters congregate in the desert.) I suppose I have become hooked on sage-grouse hunting. . . . Or, maybe it's the breathtaking scenery enjoyed without the distraction of man. And, after all, what else can you do with a pointer bird dog in September?

Can a Pointer Think?

Chapter XIV

English pointers aren't renowned for possessing the highest degree of canine intelligence; rather, their reputations derive from being aggressive and industrious hunters. One can certainly bring into question the brilliance of an animal who runs till exhausted simply to find and point a small, feathered creature. Regardless, I've seen numerous instances when they have seemed to exhibit an impressive level of reasoning power.

Spot was the first bird dog that I owned (or, more correctly, he owned me), and he knew a great deal more about quail hunting than I did, so he immediately took charge of our hunting escapades. Like most pointers, Spot never liked to retrieve, but he expected—no, he demanded—that at least one bird would be on the ground after each covey rise. Thank God, he didn't demand two! From Spot's vantage point, my sole contribution to the proceedings was to kill birds, and he concluded that I should be at least moderately proficient at this task. My level of marksmanship meant that he frequently became annoyed but usually suffered through the dry spells. However, that was not always the case.

I remember once in South Georgia there were birds everywhere, yet I couldn't hit the broad side of a barn. With the first covey rise I scored a neat double miss, then did a repeat performance with the second covey, much to Spot's disgust, and continued to produce identical results with a number of singles.

Spot's intolerance mounted. He threw me a "you'd-better-get-on-the-ball-or-else" look, as he pointed again on the edge of a peanut field. Suddenly, I developed a first-class case of "buck fever." The birds escaped into a swamp, though I tried to convince Spot that one had continued to "fly with his heart shot out."

Spot decided he'd had enough. He went on hunting, but clearly his demeanor changed radically. He pointed again in an open field. As I approached to within fifty yards, he jumped into the middle of the covey, flushed the birds, then gave me a condescending look as if to say "to hell with you." He trotted arrogantly back to our mode of transportation, a '39 Chevy, and lay down on the back seat. Despite my pleas, he refused to resume hunting—and remained aloof all the way home.

On our next trip, I did manage to wing a bird down on the first covey rise, and Spot appeared satisfied. In spite of not-infrequent episodes of poor marksmanship on my part, he never took me to task to this degree again. I'm not sure why he made up his mind on that particular trip to teach me the importance of killing birds, nor why he never repeated the lesson. He felt it sufficient, I believe, to reduce my ego to the vanishing point just one time. He knew I had learned that if I ever expected to hunt with him again, then I damned well better kill birds.

Spot could think.

A number of years ago a close friend gave me an ungainly drop named Belle, a superb bird dog. Like many of her kind, she had been force-broken to retrieve but didn't like it. I never knew Belle to ruffle a bird's feather when she dutifully retrieved, if not to hand, at least to my vicinity.

On one occasion I had hunted her hard for several days, and she was ready for a rest. Belle pointed a single at the edge of a very deep canal. The bird flushed, I fired, and it fell on the far side. Belle swam across the canal, picked up the bird, and started to return. I watched from the other side, proud as could be, and ready to praise her for being a peerless retriever.

She dipped her paw in the water and stopped. She seemed to smile, then backed up and sat down on the bank. While resting, she proceeded to eat the bird. On the opposite bank, mad as hell, my face turned crimson. Then I realized what Belle was thinking: She was impervious to punishment from me and could partake of a snack. I laughed so hard I almost fell in the water.

After Belle finished her repast, she got up, stretched leisurely, and swam back across and resumed hunting. I'm convinced that Belle knew I could not cross the canal to reprimand her, so she decided to have a lunch break. She never repeated this culinary performance, even when sleeping on a bunch of dead birds while riding home.

A small lemon-and-white pointer named Tiny acquired me several years ago. Nature didn't bless her with a particularly good nose, but with hard work and desire she developed into a more than adequate bird dog. We hunted several seasons together, then were joined by Hannah, an outstanding fifteen-month-old, liver-and-white, bird-finding machine. Hannah beat Tiny to nearly all the birds, and Tiny grew jealous, finally developing an obvious active dislike for Hannah. Still, like a pro, she accepted the less spectacular jobs of backing and retrieving.

One day Hannah winded where a covey had been feeding, and although not sure of the precise location, she pointed. Tiny arrived and backed, but no birds could be flushed. I clucked to the dogs to relocate. Tiny started trailing rapidly as if on a hot scent across the field, glancing back to make sure Hannah followed. On two occasions Tiny pointed. She continued to trail, and though Hannah behaved as if she didn't smell anything, both of us followed Tiny. After perhaps a hundred yards of this charade, Tiny suddenly wheeled and sped as fast as she could back to the original point, moved about twenty feet, and pointed the birds. Hannah and I stood, mouths agape, wondering what had happened!

I am convinced that from the start Tiny knew where the birds were and decided to lead Hannah on a merry chase out of the area so that she could return and be first on point. When the birds were flushed, Tiny shot her rival an unmistakable, "Gotcha-didn't-I?" glance.

Hannah developed into a wonderful wide-ranging dog that, once pointed, was as staunch as a rock. I used her to train younger dogs, which required that she find birds, then hold point while I taught the neophytes to point and back. At times she had to hold her point even while the younger dogs ran up birds in front of her, a most distasteful experience for Hannah. A few times, becoming thoroughly exasperated, she rolled her eyes as if to say, "To hell with this," and jumped right into the middle of the covey. This misbehavior didn't happen often, and I continued using her as a mentor. The situation could, I suppose, be compared to forcing Einstein to teach Math 101. Hannah, unknown to me, plotted to find a way out of this onerous training duty.

Most young dogs tend to follow an older dog until they learn how to hunt on their own. Hannah began enticing novices to follow her, whereupon she'd vacate the area and manage to lose her companions in a nearly impenetrable palmetto thicket or dense woods, a mile or so from where I hunted. Then Hannah would return to me, tail wagging and with a look that seemed to say, "I got rid of the nuisance, so now we can do some real hunting?" This always resulted in my wasting thirty minutes or more searching for the lost dog. Hannah eventually won this battle hands down! I stopped forcing her to train young dogs.

Can anyone say Hannah couldn't think?

When hunting on a fairly large acreage in a vehicle, it is standard practice to run two pointers for an hour or so, then rotate to another brace. But, rather than enjoying the break, the dogs much prefer hunting to riding in a truck. Faith, an enterprising genius, was no exception, and she developed several schemes to be released first. She whined a constant, high-pitched annoyance that stopped only when she got her way . . . or, as happened, when I outfitted her with a bark-suppressor collar. When she still didn't get her way, she tried a new approach. She held back her normal bowel movement until the optimal time, in order to smell up the dog box, all the while wearing an angelic expression that said, "See, if you let me hunt, this wouldn't happen." I refused to acquiesce.

When that second plan failed, she adopted a most damnable strategy. Faith had never quarreled or fought with the other dogs before, so her new plan took me by surprise. I'm certain she decided that, if the other dogs were hurt, I would have to let her hunt. Accordingly, she waited until I was away from the truck hunting, and then she macerated a front paw of the dog kenneled with her. She effectively disabled, for a week to ten days, three dogs in a short period. Faith watched kennel mates hop around on three legs, unable to hunt, and exhibited no remorse whatever. She won; thereafter she was always first on the ground.

The most notable example of pointer mentation occurred one afternoon as Joey and I hunted with a partially trained, headstrong, and incredibly stupid dog named Buck and a small setter named Rebel. The two winded a covey of birds, briefly pointed, and then one of them (I'm not sure which) flushed the quail.

It was hardly a spectacular piece of dog work. Joey grabbed Rebel, the nearest at hand, and began to get his attention with a freshly cut stalk from a cabbage tree. Rebel bemoaned his fate loudly, and Buck, perhaps knowing that his turn would come next, launched a dramatic first strike. He circled Joey, spied a brief opening, and took a huge bite out of his backside, hanging on for dear life. The look on Joey's face was priceless, assisted, no doubt, by my laughing so hard I nearly got sick.

Of course, when things straightened out, Buck received a serious attitude adjustment. My guess, however, is that throughout this procedure, he remained very pleased with himself for having given tit-for-tat. The hunt continued, but the dogs behaved in an orderly fashion. Of necessity, Joey took care over the next few days to sit down slowly.

Whether these episodes demonstrate a true ability to think, I cannot prove. I suspect that an animal psychologist would not be convinced by this evidence, but in my view, having endured more than a half century of a love-hate relationship with pointer bird dogs, I am absolutely certain that they have far more intelligence than what is usually credited to them. . . . And, yes, they can actually think.

Photographing a Bird Dog

Chapter XV

Invariably, as a cherished bird dog grows older, you wax sentimental and want tangible evidence of the good times together. But for those who can't afford to pay an artist to paint a portrait of the dog or would balk at having your faithful companion stuffed and displayed in the living room, the favored approach involves a photograph. In the keepsake picture, the dog should be on a beautiful point, standing like a statue against an idyllic background—an almost impossible task. I'm not a photographer, but I have dealt with myriad problems in trying to snap such a picture.

This epistle won't be about cameras. For my purpose, they have to be small, portable, durable, automatically focused and basically idiot-proof. You have to concentrate on posing the dog and not fiddling with the camera.

My initial experience in gun-dog photography occurred when Spot was eight to ten years old. A friend had offered the use of several pen-raised quail, a rarity at the time, and neither Spot nor I had experience with "tame" birds. It was late summer, but I figured we could place a pair of these birds in a small box covered over with broomstraw and make the setting look reasonably natural.

I'm not in the habit of exercising my dogs during the hot summer months, so when I loaded Spot into the trailer, he knew something different was up. I drove to an ideal location, placed the caged birds in a picturesque setting, and turned Spot loose. He ran around for several minutes. With camera in hand, I directed him to the birds. At a distance of fifteen feet he winded them, whirled, and pointed. Or, at least he stopped. Mouth wide open, tail halfway down, body relaxed, this great bird dog showed no style at all. He turned his head and looked at me as I approached. "What's going on?" he seemed to ask.

I had borrowed a box-type camera but hadn't bothered to learn to use it, and now I fumbled with the damn thing trying to distinguish the front from the back. While I was so engaged, Spot broke his lackadaisical pose, ambled over to the cage, looked derisively at the birds, and decided he'd had enough of this nonsense. He raised his leg, watered the area thoroughly and sped off in high gear. Laughing uncontrollably, I dropped the camera and broke it. A damper lasting several years descended on my budding career in bird dog photography.

Now, to return to the "how to" discussion of dog photography. In preparing the dog for the upcoming session, first remove all electronic paraphernalia, such as training and beeper collars; they detract from any picturesque pose. The chief obstacle in snapping a bird dog while he is pointing wild quail is seeing the subject clearly. Although everything might look perfect through the viewfinder, inevitably the developed prints will contain too much underbrush, blackberry briars, broomstraw, and not enough dog.

Another problem is positioning. Since the birds are in front of the dog, if you move in front of him, the covey will flush, whereupon the point—and the picture—will be lost. Thus, you are relegated to photographing your companion's rear-end. Frequently, the only thing in evidence will be the tail and where the tail joins the body, not really the most attractive part of a pointer's anatomy (although I admit I've grown found of this sight).

The ideal picture must show the dog's eyes. Why? To me, the "dreamlike" gaze of the pointer is the most impressive aspect of the point. But that presents another problem. To photograph the eyes, you must be in front of the dog and, thus, risk flushing the covey. To avoid this problem, my approach is to photograph the pointer while backing; this way the picture may be taken from any angle desired. When the opportunity arrives, snap the picture at once, lest the dog thinks you have become deranged, i.e., crawling around on the ground with a camera instead of shooting the birds.

Most important of all, ask this question: Why are you taking the picture? It's unlikely you'll win prizes in a photography contest. If your purpose is to one day be able to refresh your memory about the multiple good times you've had with this dog, my advice is not to be a perfectionist. Just get a picture. Don't worry if the only thing visible is the small round button beneath the tail.

A Tale of Two Litters

Chapter XVI

During my long association with pointer bird dogs, I have, with a couple of exceptions, avoided raising and training puppies. This stems from two factors: First, I really don't like to deal with the learning curve of obstreperous pointer pups, preferring to hunt with trained dogs, and second, since two to three dogs were all I needed for foot hunting, I was able to find a succession of eighteen-month, to three-year-old, partially-trained or finished bird dogs. However, things changed dramatically when I began hunting in Florida! All of a sudden, rather than two to three, I needed a minimum of eight trained dogs, and that was because of the large amount of land to be covered and the hot weather.

I tried for a time to maintain my previous approach, but the current cost and unavailability of seasoned pointers made it impossible. In addition, and very important, Joey was able to let young puppies run loose for six or seven months and develop on their own. (Pen-raised pointer puppies excel only at getting into trouble.) Thus, a new plan emerged. I would breed the bitches and raise the litter until the pups were approximately three months of age. They would go to Florida and run loose until about a year old when training in the field would begin.

This approach guaranteed that the surviving puppies would be "street smart" with regard to the multiple aspects of getting along in the woods. Also, it allowed us to pick out the best prospects. A litter from Lib II and Hank produced two excellent dogs. She had only four puppies. One was killed by a rattlesnake when quite young, and one died from eating rat poison. The other two, Luke and Faith, became outstanding dogs. In fact, taking it all in all, Faith is probably the best bird dog I've ever owned. The only drawback was that several of Lib II's kin had hypoglycemic episodes resulting in seizures. Luke was affected; Faith was not.

In order to put the plan in motion, I obtained from Jarrett Thompson an outstanding four-year-old-male, Cody (predominate breeding: Guard Rail/

Pork Roll) and a six-year-old-bitch, Missy (Whippoorwill's Rebel/Highway). Previously, it should be noted, Missy had produced several excellent dogs. I hunted them the entire season, and they performed extremely well. So the stage was set to raise two litters: Breeding Cody to both Missy and Faith.

As luck would have it, and I am usually not this lucky, both the bitches came in heat and were bred in April, with the pups due sometime around the first of July. As the time for delivery approached, they were placed in separate pens with a house designed for whelping. I was looking forward to the puppies with a great deal of expectation.

One Saturday morning in late June, I went to feed Missy and saw she was in trouble. She ran around in the pen, stopping every few seconds to lie down and strain. A quick examination revealed that she was trying to deliver, but the pup was "hung-up." I immediately drove her to a veterinarian who, by chance, was in the office. To make a long story short, at 4:00 P.M., I arrived back at home with eight healthy pups, a drowsy bitch that had just undergone a Cesarean section, a supply of artificial bitches' milk, vitamins, and a great deal of apprehension. (She actually had ten pups, but two of them died.)

Well, the first three to four days required a considerable amount of bottle nursing. Mama recovered rapidly and soon began lactating. She took over my feeding chores when the pups were about a week old. (It's amazing what pointer bird dogs can withstand.) Obviously, I spent a lot of time with these pups.

A week after Missy's litter appeared, Faith whelped six beautiful pups. She raised them by herself without any mishap. Both the litters were weaned at six weeks of age and developed rapidly. There is an interesting note about pointer pups: They are probably the most attractive creatures on earth, especially when one considers how headstrong and obnoxious they can be when reaching adulthood.

What to name them? Since I was certain that Faith would have the best litter since she was the best dog I had ever owned and had excellent bloodlines (Guard Rail/Elhew), I decided to name her pups after some of my best previous dogs. Hence, Sandy, Lemon, Cricket, Belle, Spot, and Tiny were duly christened. By then I had about run out of names, so I thought it might be at least unusual to name Missy's litter after Shakespearean characters. My perverse nature also came into play, as I thought it would be fun to listen to Joey, in his South Florida cracker brogue, yelling Hor-a-tio or Ham-let! At any rate, Horatio, Hamlet, Humphrey, Prince Hal, Miranda, Kate, Portia, and Cordelia were suitably identified.

In spite of my prior notion that Faith's puppies would be the best, by the time they were ten weeks old, it became clear that Missy's were far more aggressive, playful, and all-round better dogs. In fact, I couldn't find fault with any of them, except that Cordelia was somewhat retiring and did not like to be petted. Faith's litter just didn't have the same spunk.

The pups survived Hurricane Fran, with pine trees falling in the pen, and came through unscathed. They made the trip to Florida in October, suitably immunized and de-wormed. Joey allowed them to run about and play, first in groups of four to five and then later on in groups of two or three. By the time quail season arrived in early December, it was very clear that Missy's puppies were by far the best. Joey indicated to me that they were the most eager and impressive young pointers he had ever seen. Certainly, they were quite adept at destroying the flower gardens, chasing birds, and generally getting into mischief.

For the next six months, only one tragedy occurred: Sandy was killed on the road. The rest continued to grow and develop, hunting on their own and generally having a good time. One day, during the later part of the bird season, Joey was hunting in the preserve approximately 1½ miles from where the pups were kenneled. He was hunting with one dog when all of a sudden he found two other dogs pointing. Portia and Horatio had joined the hunt and were pointing the birds. The client shot, and Portia and Horatio left forthwith to hunt for another covey. This scenario was repeated on several occasions by Missy's pups.

During the spring, we had to make a disposition regarding training. I elected to bring Hal, Horatio, and Miranda home with me for obedience and retriever training. Portia, Tiny, Kate, and Cricket went to a preserve owner who was a friend of Joey's on a two-for-one basis (we gave him two dogs to train, and one would be returned). A similar arrangement was made with another trainer for Hamlet, Humphrey, Belle, and Cordelia. Another friend of Joey's swapped the training of Lemon for a bull calf. Spot developed neurologic difficulties—an inoperable brain tumor—and Belle began to have seizures after minimal exercise. Both had to be culled.

The three that I brought home were the easiest-handling and most-rapidly-progressing pups that I have owned. They were very easy to teach to "Whoa" and to retrieve.

When the next season started, the three dogs that I had worked began hunting with almost no problems. However, Miranda did not have the same drive as the two males. Portia and Tiny came back to Joey well started; Hamlet and Humphrey came back only partially started.

By the later part of the quail season, it was quite obvious that Missy's litter was outstanding and that we had a superior group of dogs. Horatio, Hamlet, Portia, and Humphrey were superb in all regards. Unfortunately, Hal began flagging especially when pointing single birds. Miranda, as noted above, was not as aggressive as the others. The preserve owner thought Kate was excellent, although not as good as Portia. He judged Cricket to be OK. We came to the same conclusion with Tiny—adequate only. Cordelia remained aloof and was sold. Lemon never progressed and seemed to have little or no hunting ability or desire to hunt quail. He became a mediocre hog dog. (I hope that the bull traded for Lemon's training performed better.)

So there we are. Faith's puppies, clearly in my mind, were to be the best. From this litter, only two were judged as adequate, but neither came close to being as good as their mother. In contrast, Missy produced five outstanding dogs and two that are a lot better than average. Why? I have no idea. Both litters had the same father. They were raised and trained exactly the same way. Unquestionably, the superior breeding qualities of the bitch made the difference.

On the other hand, another variable must be considered . . . my bottle-feeding of Missy's litter. Perhaps I'm responsible?!

Several episodes with these young dogs stand out in my memory. Shortly after being released and before emptying out, Horatio pointed with a picturesque stance. As I watched him, I saw his rear-end gradually drop down as he started his daily constitutional. His front-end never moved. When the business was over, he resumed his stylish point.

Early on, Hal liked to run at top speed, especially after a covey flushed. He didn't exactly chase the birds but ran in a big circle, returning in two to three minutes. I killed a bird that fell in the open. As he returned from his travels, he smelled the bird, picked it up, and returned to me without slowing down.

Hamlet did not emulate his Shakespearean namesake in being indecisive. Even at a young age, he seemed to run from one covey to the next without effort and little, if any, trailing—just pointing. One day he pointed a released quail that had perched on the motor of the swamp buggy. Hamlet's back legs were on the ground. His front legs were on the tire, but he held a staunch point!

On our annual trip to Wyoming, the first time that Missy's family saw sage grouse, they acted like professionals. With the exception of Horatio, deciding that he must hunt two to three miles from where we were, they all found and held sage grouse. It is extremely unusual for young dogs to be so talented!

I'm not sure which is the best: Hamlet, Horatio, or Portia, but all three are big-going, stylish, and smart dogs. Humphrey is a close fourth, with Hal and Miranda way better than average. Kate is considered a brag dog by her owner.

What else can I say? Since I plagiarized the title of this story from Dickens, perhaps I should end the same way. 'Tis a far, far better litter that I have now than I have seen before.

Neutering—Nonsense or Not?

Chapter XVII

For many years my female pointers have been spayed unless I plan to breed them. Not having to deal with bitches in heat, which invariably occurs at the beginning of the quail season, is reason enough for the operation. As best I can tell, there are no negative consequences. The widely held notion that spaying a female will make her lazy is unfounded. Rena, Hannah, Tiny, Anne, etc., were all "powerhouses."

On the other hand, for unclear reasons, probably a "macho thing," I never had entertained the concept of neutering the males. In fact, due to the propensity for male pointers to fight, I have owned only a few. When I met Joey, he had a number of pointers that had been castrated to obviate the tendency to fight. To be as kind as possible, these dogs ranked as average to worthless but . . . they did not fight. I ascribed their inadequacy to the neutering rather than the more obvious fact that they were sorry to begin with.

My first experience with neutering one of my male dogs was with Luke, an excellent bird dog but unfit for breeding because of seizures. I decided to have him castrated. Not only were there no deleterious effects, he actually improved. Luke concentrated only on bird hunting. No time was spent "marking" every bush or chasing females about to come into heat during the next month. Also, fighting had no part of his makeup.

With this good result, I made the decision to neuter all but one of the year-old males from Missy's litter. After considerable discussion, Joey and I decided that Hal should be kept as a stud dog. This choice wasn't easy because both Hamlet and Horatio were super dogs as well. Since Joey was adept at performing the operation, we planned for him to proceed.

I didn't hear from him for several days, but I finally received a telephone call. In a rather sheepish manner, he told me that he had "made a mistake." Hal was neutered while Hamlet remained intact.

I'm certain that Joey expected me to become quite angry. When I began laughing, he couldn't understand the humor. I explained to him that from now on, no matter what miscue I was guilty of, there was no way that he would ever be able to criticize me. I was "one-up" on him forever. On the other hand, Hal didn't seem to be quite so sanguine about the situation. Several days later, Joey received the following letter.

April 17, 1998
Mr. Joey O'Bannon
8400 SW Fox Brown Rd.
Indiantown, FL 34956

Dear Mr. O'Bannon:

How could you! This level of incompetence reaches a new low. I had looked forward to performing the duties of a stud dog since my father had informed me how much fun was involved. You certainly ended that career!

Throughout our relationship, I have tried my best to become a good bird dog. Admittedly, I was somewhat nervous when you came up behind me while I was on point and undoubtedly moved more than I should have. You ain't seen nothing yet! There is no way that I will ever allow you to approach me from the rear again.

I am trying to be philosophical regarding your dastardly deed and will continue to try to be an outstanding bird dog. However, I can assure you, if the opportunity presents itself, you will have a new name—"No-Nuts O'Bannon."

I do hope that with time I can overcome my deep sense of shame and humiliation, but, as for now, I remain pissed-off!

Your former friend,

Prince Hal (now Princess Hallie)

P.S. The lawyer at the Canine Legal Defense Fund told me that if there ever was a case of sexual harassment, this is it. I hope your liability insurance is paid up!

In the intervening years, Hal has regained his lost sense of pride. However, Hamlet, Horatio, and Humphrey all have turned out to be much better dogs than Hal who developed the bad habit of flagging. Also, Hamlet recently sired a litter of excellent puppies. Although Joey recently has tried to claim credit for making the correct decision, I won't let him get away with it. Undoubtedly, Divine guidance was working in his favor.

In the Good Ole Summertime—George vs. Pepper

Chapter XVIII

The long hiatus from the end of one quail season to the beginning of the next is always a period of moderate to severe depression for a true bird hunter. I am no exception.

On the other hand, I take care of the bird dogs myself and have a day-by-day interaction with them. Their general demeanor in the pen teaches me a lot about a bird dog. I am not trying to tout pointers as lovable companions; they are not. But, they can be fun to interact with, even in the off-season. Also, if needed, I can re-emphasize retrieving and be certain that they respond correctly to "Come here" and "Whoa." This daily interaction is helpful in developing a close relationship that comes to fruition during the hunting season. Also, I just like to be around bird dogs.

This particular episode concerns the interplay between a Canadian goose (George) and an English setter (Pepper), which took place over a number of months, culminating in a rather dramatic conclusion.

George arrived on the scene first. In 1970, I purchased twenty-eight acres of land surrounded by the much larger Duke Forest. A two-acre lake was soon constructed, along with a cabin and pens for my dogs. After a couple of years, I decided to obtain two, pinioned Canadian geese. In due course, George and his mate arrived. Over the course of the next three to four years they dutifully raised two to four young geese each year.

Upon arrival, George took control of the pond and assumed that it was his to protect. In fact, he soon became a real "guard goose." He was somewhat of a nuisance when he pecked and flailed at my legs with his wings, but I learned to push him away rather forcefully with my foot. We developed a reasonable standoff relationship; however, visitors to the area had to be warned of George's pugnacious attitude.

One day George attacked the thirteen-year-old grandson of one of my fox-hunting friends while he was out fishing. The young man became so frightened that he dove headfirst into the pond. I had to quickly vanquish George and retrieve the bedraggled boy, covered with mud. He completely lost interest in fishing.

Another most memorable event regarding "guard goose" George occurred one beautiful summer day. I was resting quietly, my back against a tree, and enjoying the peaceful surroundings when a young couple arrived, blanket in hand, planning to have a picnic. They were unaware of my presence. Although my land was posted to ward off strangers, I never enforced this rule and decided to leave them alone. The couple spread the blanket on the other side of the lake and sat down. A few minutes later, George decided to intervene. The next thing I knew, he had attacked the picnicking couple, and I can still remember the loud screams as the young lady in question ran through the woods with George in hot pursuit . . . pecking at her rear-end. They did not return. I became the new owner of the blanket.

George never went near the dog pens. However, one spring, instead of building their nest near the lake, he and his mate used the roof of a small out-building near the dog pen as a nesting site. Thus, George became a frequent visitor to the dog pens. He didn't like them, and they didn't like him. The two pointer females, Tiny and Gypsy, were housed in one pen, and Pepper, my only setter, was kenneled in the next. The pens were constructed of two-by-four welded wire fencing.

Two to three times a day, George would demonstrate near the pen by hissing and running toward the fence with an outstretched neck. His actions caused Tiny and Gypsy to bark hysterically and "cuss" at George while trying to get at him from their side of the fence. On the other hand, Pepper remained aloof, watching the proceedings but never becoming openly demonstrative. Pepper's attitude really made George mad. He expended considerable effort to try to solicit a response from Pepper. (I could tell by Pepper's eyes, however, that he was far from detached—"jus layin' low," waiting for an opening.) This general scenario continued for several weeks.

I had imagined that when the goslings were hatched, the family would repair to the lake and not continue the interaction with the dogs, but that was not the case. George and his mate continued parading themselves and their young near the dog pen at least twice daily to the consternation of all the dogs. When the young geese got close to the pen, it would excite both the pointers and George to a frenzied pitch—they barking and growling and he hissing and demonstrating. Pepper still remained detached and seemingly disinterested. (But I could tell George had better watch out!)

I wasn't around when the final Armageddon occurred, so I can only relate the results. Late one afternoon, I went to check on the bird dogs. There was George next to Pepper's pen. There was a problem. George's head was no longer attached to his body! I looked at Pepper, and Pepper looked at me with a contented smirk. Then he went into his house and brought the head back for my inspection. (Pepper was a good retriever.) Well, what could I do? George really brought the decapitation upon himself. Dejectedly, I gathered George's head and body and disposed of his remains.

This episode was not followed by subsequent adverse bird dog/goose interactions. Although the geese occasionally walk by the pen, they ignore the dogs and vice-versa.

The young geese grew up. In fact, George's sons and daughters and their prodigy, along with a number of other nonmigratory Canadian geese, are becoming a nuisance. This summer I had nearly thirty-five geese utilizing the lake for a residence.

I'm not sure whether this story has a moral. If so, it might be, "Don't lose your head in a meaningless squabble."

In Sickness and in Health

Chapter XIX

Obviously, assuring that one's bird dogs are in excellent health and condition is a key component to successful bird hunting. Even more, the bird dogs who own me insist that I provide the best "health care coverage." Over the years I've been extraordinarily lucky with them and have had to deal with only a few significant illnesses.

As with the treatment of disease in man, the advances in veterinary medicine over the past thirty years have been extraordinary. Currently, it is relatively easy to maintain a hunting dog, parasite free and immunized against many of the fatal infectious diseases.

Such was not always the case. For example, heartworms used to be a major problem. Prevention was essentially nonexistent, and the treatment, while effective, had multiple significant side effects. In the late 1960s, I acquired a female pointer that, while not outstanding, was at least acceptable. Much to my dismay, I soon discovered that she had heartworms. At that time, the treatment consisted of giving an arsenic-containing compound intravenously. It worked. However, there was a major side effect; her sense of smell essentially disappeared. (A bird dog that cannot smell is not a prized possession.)

Skin diseases caused by fleas, ticks, and occasionally mange were treated by immersing the dog in a mixture of burnt motor oil, flowers of sulfur, and carbolic acid. What a mess! Worm infestation, especially the difficult-to-eradicate whip worms, resulted in significant debilitation in adult dogs. Nowadays these maladies are easily, albeit expensively, either treated or prevented.

By far the most common significant health problems are those caused by trauma—specifically, significant lacerations and injuries occurring while hunting or in the case of male pointers, while fighting. Most of these I dealt with myself with needle and thread.

However, when Anne had her left eye seriously injured by a palmetto bush, she lost the ability to see in both eyes. Luckily, the North Carolina Veterinary School is nearby, and several excellent veterinary ophthalmologists are on the staff. They removed one eye and restored vision in the other. Anne came home with a brand new glass eye. The veterinarian thought it would be cosmetically unacceptable to do otherwise. Well fine! Anne was clearly the ugliest bird dog I ever owned, and a $1,000 artificial eye really didn't make her more attractive.

One of the more interesting results from trauma occurred recently with Cody. As with many male bird dogs, Cody missed no opportunity to get into a confrontation with another dog, and for a couple of weeks before I arrived in Florida, he had been successful. It took Joey O'Bannon several minutes to separate the contestants, and Cody's right ear was severely bruised. There did not appear to be any significant *sequelae*, and we assumed Cody was ready to go hunting.

Cody, a wide-ranging dog, maintains an excellent forward pattern and responds readily to a whistle. On this occasion, however, Cody appeared to be hunting entirely on his own and soon became lost. I realized something was amiss when I saw him about three hundred yards away and blew the whistle, which he clearly heard. However, instead of coming in my direction, Cody ran the other way. Like people, bird dogs sometimes have bad days. I put Cody up, figuring by the next day he would decide to be part of the team.

But the next day the situation got worse. Being a somewhat slow learner, it took me awhile to decipher the problem; I should have done so earlier. Since I hear very poorly out of my right ear and, hence, cannot determine the direction from which sounds come, it suddenly occurred to me that Cody might be similarly afflicted. I examined him and found that the right ear was swollen to the point that the canal was closed—the results of the previous fight. With treatment it took about a week or so for the swelling to disappear, and he returned to his former behavior.

While treating a variety of canine maladies over the years, the response of the "patient" can vary markedly. Some dogs like attention; some dogs don't. Pepper (my only setter) fell into the former category. The summer after Pepper joined my contingent, he became listless and his belly swelled with fluid. Diagnosis: Very severe infestation with heartworms causing heart failure. The treatment required a number of intravenous infusions during the course of two to three weeks. He had to be kept isolated and not allowed to exert himself at all; in other words, he was "spoiled rotten." Pepper did fine, and soon the heartworms were gone. However, he remembered the process and missed all the attention. Periodically, over the next few years, he would feign illness when nothing was wrong. This charade was clearly an attention-getting mechanism—so much so that I dubbed similar behavior in other dogs as "pulling a Pepper."

By far the most unusual and interesting health problem occurred in one of my fox hounds. Because I fox hunt primarily at night, the hounds would come back to the point where they had been released early the next day. One morning, Percy, a Walker fox hound, was late in returning. He arrived about 10:00 A.M. and, I must say, gave every evidence of having been involved with something long dead. He stank to "high heaven." (This behavior is not uncommon in hunting dogs.) I loaded Percy into the truck and thought little about it, except being thankful that I could ride in the cab and not have to smell the results of his indiscretions.

When I got back at the kennel around 2:00 P.M., something clearly was amiss. Percy was markedly unsteady, his tail was drooping, and his eyelids were nearly closed. The situation deteriorated, and by that evening he couldn't stand up. It was obvious that Percy had ingested the wrong thing. The next morning, his condition was unchanged, but at least he was able to breathe normally. It soon became quite evident that Percy had paralysis due to botulism.

Botulism in dogs is rare, but Type C occurs, usually secondary to eating contaminated chickens. (I found out later that Percy had found where a number of chickens had been thrown in the woods.) In dogs, botulism is called "coon dog paralysis."

Paralyzed to the point that he could swallow only liquids, Percy obviously required a lot of care. His condition remained unchanged for nearly a month, but he gradually improved and became able to eat and drink normally.

I discussed botulism with several of my colleagues in the Infectious Diseases Division at Duke. They had never seen an example of this disease (botulism is extraordinarily uncommon in humans) and were extremely interested in Percy's malady. In fact, Percy, his disease, and his well being became a frequent point of discussion in the Medical Center.

Medical Grand Rounds at Duke is a semiformal weekly conference in which a patient with an interesting clinical problem is presented in detail to an audience of a hundred or more physicians. When possible, the patient is present to answer questions about the specific disease process. Well, guess what? Percy made an appearance at Medical Grand Rounds, suitably attired for the occasion and resting on a stretcher. Needless to say, he didn't answer questions, but he did demonstrate the paralysis caused by *Clostridium botulinum* toxin. Percy's "performance" was by far the most memorable Grand Rounds presentation that year.

Percy gradually improved and in about six weeks was finally able to stand up. Two months later, he returned to hunting, although his eyelids remained permanently droopy.

So much for health problems.

However, there is a final, somewhat somber note. What to do when a bird dog becomes unable to hunt either due to old age or a debilitating injury? Certainly, as they grow older, bird dogs are unable to be "top dog" but can still turn in a credible performance. However, what I am describing is a situation whereby they deteriorate further and can no longer hunt effectively. Early on, I used to "let nature take its course," but it became obvious that leaving a dog whining in the pen and wanting to hunt was not an acceptable answer. I could not allow my hunting companions to suffer such an injustice, so I decided to forthrightly deal with the issue myself.

It's not easy, when we both know "the time" has finally arrived. Since I have been dealing with bird dogs for more than five decades, this situation has been all too frequent. I am continually addressing the question as to why a dog can't have a similar life span as a human. There is a very quiet and solemn place on a hill near my home where, upon occasion, I go alone and sit. . . . . I think about the past, surrounded by my former companions. As expected, most of these thoughts involve hunting experiences (many detailed in this book), but surprisingly, individual quirks and eccentric behavior in the pen frequently are remembered as well.

Some of my dogs' most memorable eccentricities include Anne, who while waiting to be fed, always jumped up and turned completely around while still in the air. Good table manners are not usually a component of a pointer's makeup; in fact, they devour all the food in a few rapid gulps. Faith, for example, was a champion glutton. Tiny, however, always ate slowly and in a prissy fashion, just like a "lady," which she was. Pepper, I guess to amuse himself, continually ran a figure-eight pattern in the pen. For five or six hours each day, Hank jumped vertically three or four feet high at the gate. (These exercises kept both Pepper and Hank in tiptop shape.)

I could go on *ad nauseam*, but it should be obvious that I have a lot of wonderful memories. I hope that wherever they are, the dogs think of me occasionally . . . and someday, just maybe, we'll hunt together again.

Pepper

Pepper, you've come to the end of the chase,
And it's up to me to end your race.
For eight great years I've watched you run,
Point, and back; ready for the gun.
From Carolina's thicket to Florida's swale,
We've hunted together for Bobwhite quail.
I've seen you trail from scent so faint,
The other dogs must stop and wait.
You've made me swear countless times
By hunting your way instead of mine.
But all in all, you've proven to be
As fine a setter as I hope to see.
Now you're old and ready to try
To hold a running covey in the sky.
I hope some day to find you there,
Pointing birds, not moving a hair.
So let's walk to where the others rest,
And I'll start you on this Heavenly quest.
When you're gone, I'll ask Him again —
Why must a dog's life be shorter than men?
(1990)

Where Did All the Wild Quail Go?

Chapter XX

Not long ago, I hunted unsuccessfully in an ideal quail venue near Hobe Sound, Florida. It is a ranch that is covered with a sprinkling of pine trees, low bush palmettos, gallberries, ground acorns, wild grass, and a variety of seed-bearing weeds. Low areas usually contain ponds filled with water, except in very dry times.

About eighty Brahma cattle graze the twenty-seven hundred acres, and for the past three years the land had been methodically burned and opened up to facilitate quail propagation. The ranch was posted, and no one but myself hunted birds there. When the previous hunting season ended, at least fifteen coveys of birds called the ranch home, and throughout the summer numerous pairs of quail with young were regularly spotted.

In October, a tropical storm struck, and twenty-four inches of water suddenly covered the land. When the flood receded, the quail had disappeared. Currently, I am trying to develop several strategies to repopulate the birds, each of which is time-consuming and expensive. Even if I don't give up on the project, it will take a number of years.

Regardless, a flood, followed by the absence of birds, provides a reasonable cause-and-effect explanation as to why the quail are missing. While not particularly gratifying, the solution to the mystery is evident. What takes deeper probing is learning why the quail population has been decreasing everywhere.

Historically, quail populations cycle significantly, primarily because of weather conditions and possibly disease. However, all the places where I had hunted birds successfully in the past experienced a severe reduction in the number of quail, starting in the early 1980s. Degradation of habitat, excessive hunting, use of pesticides, and a burgeoning number of predators have all have been implicated in this disastrous turn of events.

Habitat degradation for quail actually began and rapidly accelerated during the early 1950s when farming practices in much of the lower South changed from the tenant-farmer system to clean farming. Previously, the acreages tended by sharecropper farmers living on the land consisted of small crop fields with wide edges covered in weeds. Fallow land was rotated and planted with cover crops like lespedeza, and unfarmed ground was burned each year to control underbrush.

The tenant farmers kept chickens, guineas, etc., and thus waged a consistent war against predators: hawks, owls, snakes, raccoons, and opossums. Quail thrived under such an arrangement. But with the consolidation of farms and the development of "clean" farming, larger acreages were planted in single fields with no edges, and the sharecroppers moved away. Woods grew up into thick tangles, and the practice of burning ceased. Therefore, quail had no place to raise their young and nothing to eat. Exit quail.

By the mid-1960s, that's pretty much the way things were in the lower South. Still, although markedly reduced in numbers, quail survived and learned to adapt in the woods or on overgrown marginal land.

I began hunting North Carolina's Piedmont region during the 1960s, and although the bigger-is-better farming process had taken hold to some extent, land usage had not changed as dramatically as farther South. There had never been the practice of yearly burning. The woods primarily consisted of second-growth pine and mature hardwoods containing dense honeysuckle thickets.

In 1970, I acquired a small (twenty-eight acres) tract of wooded land surrounded by several thousand acres of forest and bordered by a power line right-of-way planted in bicolor lespedeza. Two coveys of birds used the power line. Another covey in the woods frequented a dry streambed and survived quite well on acorns. I immediately saw that I could improve the situation and planted four feed patches of approximately one-half acre each. The feed patches consisted of yearly plantings of mixed seed (provided by the State Agriculture Department) and permanent bicolor lespedeza.

By the late 1970s, I had four established coveys that no one hunted but me, and I made sure to leave no less than six birds per covey. This happy situation remained stable for several years but then began to deteriorate. Only two coveys remained in 1983, and by 1985 there were none.

Since 1985, there have been no resident quail, despite my multiple efforts to restock. The habitat, except for those "improvements" I made, has remained unchanged. No pesticides were used, nor have I or anyone else hunted the birds excessively. What happened? Throughout much of the range I hunted in Piedmont North Carolina, a similar major decrease in the number of quail also occurred.

One of my favorite spots did suffer from over-hunting. I watched with disgust when I saw an eight-quail covey, which was huddled beside a road, get killed on the ground by a meat "hunter." However, overhunting did not explain the overall decrease either, and I continued to look for answers.

The region's only crops were tobacco and a few soybeans. Although tobacco is heavily poisoned (I saw several quail die from eating poisoned hornworms), clearly this didn't count as a major factor in quail depopulation. Much of the land previously planted in tobacco had been taken out of production in the early 1970s, and the majority of tobacco farming had moved to eastern North Carolina. The former tobacco land either became scrub forest or was planted in small grains or pasture.

The quail population hit rock bottom in 1985. Since then, there has been an occasional slight upsurge but, by and large, over much of their former range, quail have mainly disappeared or have been drastically reduced in number.

The number of deer exploded, and so did the number of hunters. Still, except for a few coveys lost to ground shooting, excessive hunting of quail didn't account for their scarcity.

I have a low opinion of deer. They are animals that have benefited undeservedly from good press, generated by the fictional Bambi. In fact, I have formulated a hypothesis (probably not supportable) that the booming deer population ate the quail. If this contention is incorrect, however, I think we ought to look seriously at the deleterious work of real predators as a prime cause.

In the classic treatise *The Bob White Quail—Its Habits, Preservation And Increase*, author Herbert L. Stoddard indicated that only Cooper's and Sharp-shinned hawks posed a major danger to quail. Other hawks were deemed beneficial because they killed the enemies of quail, like rats and snakes.

The studies Stoddard relied on were carried out in the Thomasville-Tallahassee region of South Georgia-North Florida during the 1920s and early 1930s. My guess is that the conclusions were correct for that time and place; however, having spent considerable time in that region, if slightly later, I can attest to the presence of a constant war to eliminate all winged predators. Thus, the total number of hawks in the region was small. The .22 Hornet became a popular cartridge because of the ability to kill hawks at a farther range than the

.22 long rifle. Farmers firmly believed that all hawks were chicken killers and that "The only good hawk is a dead hawk."

This approach to avian predator control vanished in the early 1970s as hawks and owls were afforded legal protection. Heavy fines were levied on anyone caught killing them. Although hunters occasionally still shoot a few hawks and associated feathered relatives, these predators have geometrically increased in the past ten years. Driving on Interstates 40 and 95 recently, I counted twenty-two hawks (one approximately every ten miles) sitting in trees along the road. On my small farm, I hear great-horned or barred owls every night, and I see red-tailed and Cooper's hawks frequently.

Most hunters blame foxes for the absence of quail, but in my experience the number of foxes has been fairly static in the last fifteen years. I don't think they pose nearly the problem to quail as do their feathered enemies. Many recent studies* support the contention that hawk predation is the prime factor in decimating both wild and released birds.

I question whether significant predation is caused solely by two species, as Stoddard alleged. It is known that most avian predators readily adapt to the "easy pickings" presented by released quail on hunting preserves. I have a difficult time convincing myself that a marsh hawk with a quail in its talons isn't at least some threat to the quail population.

What can or should be done to rejuvenate the quail population? Natural disaster, of course, can't be avoided, but continued habitat destruction must be stopped. Excessive hunting can be eliminated. These two measures alone would be markedly beneficial. However, reducing the plague of avian predators also is of prime importance. Introducing "Harry the Hawk" to a high velocity .22-caliber bullet would seem, at least to me, a reasonable approach. Unfortunately, it ain't legal!

*Studies conducted by T. De Vos and D. W. Speake and reported in *Quail Unlimited*, January–February 1996.

Quail Ain't Predictable Any More

Chapter XXI

Fifty years ago finding quail was not difficult. A covey "hung out" year after year in the same place. As a young man, I frequently identified coveys by specific locations, and names such as the following come to mind: Old House Covey (a pile of rubble that once had been a home); Dead Mule Covey (immortalized the whitened remains of one of man's stubborn compatriots); and Graveyard Covey (quail frequently located near family cemeteries, perhaps to commune with the departed, but more than likely because of the small gravel usually found on these plots).

In general, these venues were characterized by nearby water, an abundant supply of food, and relatively open cover, so the birds didn't have to forage any distance to obtain life's necessities. Because they were so predictably found in the same place, an experienced meat dog soon learned these birdy places and hustled from one covey to another without bothering with the intervening land. Hunters who expected a bird dog to cover ground methodically found this habit, although productive, to be exasperating and either hunted the territory from a different direction or, infrequently, so that the dog wouldn't remember the covey's precise location. On the other hand, if hunting with a mediocre bird dog (the prototypical English setter comes to mind), the hunter might find quail by strolling from one known location to another, primarily employing the dog as a retriever or as a companion with whom to share lunch.

It bears repeating that small-time farming practices encouraged an abundant quail population. Where I hunted in middle and South Georgia, farms largely consisted of small fields planted in cotton, corn, and soybeans. Edges and fallow land were covered with weeds and other seed-bearing plants. Yearly burning kept woods and underbrush under control. Farmers practiced predator control to feed the family, or often as a sport.

Still, even in those bygone days, quail frequented some inexplicable locations. One of my favorite coveys took up residence in and around an old outdoor privy that was sheltered by a large fig tree. (I don't know why it was a common practice to plant figs next to an outhouse, but the result has been my inability to develop a taste for fig preserves.) The only cover was provided by a stack of old rusted tin roofing, a few weeds, and a surfeit of broomstraw. The surrounding land was open pasture. I have never understood the attraction of this location nor exactly what the birds ate. Yet there they were, year after year.

Habitat has greatly changed—and not for the better where quail are concerned. Clean farming has all but eliminated the small fields and edges, and the cessation of annual burning has allowed the woods and fallow land to grow into dense and impenetrable cover. These changes, coupled with the explosion in the number of critters who dine on quail, reduced their population drastically. To survive, the few remaining birds have adapted by foraging farther and by changing their requirements for both food and cover. When flushed, these "super quail" have even learned to employ a variety of different escape strategies.

Several years ago I persuaded a local farmer to leave a few rows of unharvested soybeans on the edge of a fifty-acre field. Thus, we had created adequate feed, though the cover was sparse. Pasture surrounded three-quarters of this field; the rest was bordered by woods and a fairly broad stream surrounding a twenty-by-forty-foot island, which was covered with briars and honeysuckle.

I hunted in this field three or four times, finding nary a bird, but before conceding failure I decided to give it one more chance. I brought along Cricket, a small, headstrong pointer with a propensity to hunt in overgrown cover, and she decided to check out the island. At best, Cricket had a mediocre nose, and though she may have sensed something on the island, I doubt it. Anyway, she swam perhaps twenty feet across the intervening stream, scrambled up the bank, took four or five steps, and froze on a solid point.

Whatever failings Cricket had, being unsteady was not one of them. She would have remained on point until dark. The stream wasn't particularly deep, and with the help of several rocks and a log to step on, I made it to the island with just one boot filled with water—all the while muttering that no woodcock, the most likely quarry, was worth even one wet foot.

Prepared to shoot a woodcock, I walked to Cricket. Suddenly, eight or ten quail took flight. I managed to bring down two of them; the others escaped to the far bank. After Cricket retrieved both birds, I prepared to re-cross the stream. To my surprise, Cricket pointed again on another part of the island. This time I felt sure she'd found a woodcock, or maybe a single, but, unbelievably, fourteen or fifteen quail flushed in front of her, flying across the stream. I killed one bird, which fell into the water, and Cricket made a nice retrieve. Re-crossing the stream, I filled both boots with water but paid this inconvenience no attention. Wet feet couldn't dampen my spirits.

As I remember, I killed two or three more singles that afternoon. The day had changed from a "water haul" into a memorable hunt. Obviously, there had been plenty of feed to support two bevies of birds, and they had set up housekeeping on the island because it contained the only available cover. The birds flew over to the soybeans, filled up, and then returned to their safe haven.

A favorite Durham County hunting spot of mine featured several five-acre, fallow fields. They contained a border of weeds and beggar's lice that surrounded a two-acre tobacco patch and a small section of mature forest. Here, I could always find a covey of birds feeding in the fallow land and roosting in the honeysuckle. One year in October, the owner plowed all the fields. When I arrived to hunt, I found nothing but a clean field and a few acres in open woods that contained an occasional honeysuckle thicket; obviously, there was no place for quail.

Mistletoe grew on several of the oaks, and since Christmas approached, I decided to shoot down a few bunches for decorations. Though I had planned to keep the dogs in the truck, they whined, so I turned them loose. Soon they were frozen at the base of a large oak tree containing the mistletoe. There on the ground I saw two birds, and when I walked up, a covey of ten to twelve flushed. The one I shot had a crop full of acorns.

I found the same covey on several occasions that year. They fed exclusively on acorns. The next year weeds again covered the land, and the quail went back to their previous "normal" lifestyle. I never found them in the oaks again. Clearly, that one year, they'd had two choices: Live on acorns . . . or perish. A maxim: Quail are a ground bird, rarely flying, usually walking to feed, always roosting on the ground.

One day as I hunted through an open hardwood forest, containing almost no ground cover and located between two fields where corn had been mechanically harvested, Gypsy suddenly pointed. A dog with unusual habits (which included barking when quail flushed), she pointed directly at a ten-foot-high, thick cedar tree. As I came abreast of the tree, a covey flew over my head, startling me so that I neglected to shoot. While I'd seen flushed birds fly into trees, especially when snow covered the ground, I had never seen nor heard of a covey roosting in a cedar tree. It defied established lore.

I thought perhaps they had been chased by a hawk and flew into the tree to hide. Upon examining the ground, however, I could tell from the many droppings that the covey had used the tree as a roosting site. On several occasions thereafter, I flushed the same covey from the same tree.

Although I subscribe somewhat to the notion that any quail obnoxious enough to fly into a tree should be eliminated, I killed only two birds from this covey. They continued to thrive, using the cedar tree as a roost and feeding on the corn left by the mechanical picker. The lack of ground cover, I assume, forced the birds to become arboreal.

Besides being prolific, as a primary survival strategy, quail have developed several effective approaches to escape from predators, including human hunters. They freeze, remaining immobile and undetectable for a long period, and if flushed, they fly as a unit to safety. When flushing, the birds fly almost simultaneously—a genuine heart-stopping experience to behold. This action confuses any predator and causes many hunters to become overly excited, with the result that the only thing hit is a pine tree.

On the other hand, one of the prime reasons for hunting quail is the unparalleled thrill of the covey rise. Perhaps they might be left alone if they learned not to provide the bird hunter with such an exhilarating performance. Let's hope they don't become too educated!

I have often wondered how quail, scattered over a fifty-foot radius, know to flush at the same time. If they communicate with one another, it's not audible to human ears. Perhaps ESP scientists should explore the phenomenon. My own theory is more mundane, and I believe that when the first bird leaves the ground, the reflexes of the rest are so attuned that they follow within milliseconds, giving the impression of a simultaneous flush.

I have heard in bygone days that birds, when flushed, flew a few hundred yards, glided into a broomstraw field, and waited resignedly for the bird dogs to find them individually. I think this situation occurred mainly in the minds of outdoor sports writers who never hunted. Certainly, such birds now are extinct.

The surviving quail have developed imaginative methods of escape. Even in adequate cover, few birds remain stationary after alighting. Instead, they run to the closest impenetrable thicket. Another trick a covey of quail employs when flushed is to fly in a certain direction till out of sight, and then they change course significantly. (After shooting at the covey, I usually walk in the direction they fly, even if I don't plan to hunt singles. It's not uncommon for the dogs to find an unsuspected wounded bird.)

I remember the dogs pointing a Florida covey on the edge of a narrow cypress bay. The birds flew off in the direction of a fairly open field. This happened several times, but nary a single could be found in this field. One day while starting off toward the field, I saw a covey alight not fifty yards from where the flush had occurred. At first I thought these must be different birds and unsuccessfully hunted the area where I believed the original covey went down. But these were the original birds. By the time I realized the elusive covey had circled the bay and returned almost to the point of origin, the sun had set.

I returned a few weeks later, and the birds tried the same escape tactic, but not quite so successfully that time. Fool me, would they? I showed them!

The most memorable escape tactic I have witnessed occurred several years ago while I was hunting single birds with my pointer, Mack. In Mack's younger days, he had been a better-than-average bird finder but an unwilling backer. It took numerous admonishments to make him perform the task dutifully. To avoid retribution, he grew so proficient at backing that on occasion he would back a cow, a chicken, or even a stump. I believe he enjoyed showing that he had become a sensitive, if not a specific, backer.

Anyway, I spotted Mack ahead of me, pointing at what I assumed to be a single bird. When I arrived, I saw an old ceramic slop jar turned upside down in a honeysuckle thicket. I walked through the vines, but nothing flushed. Mack held his point. I figured he was backing the jar. To prove his folly (undoubtedly he reckoned the jar was another dog), I turned the jar over with my foot. To my astonishment, out flew two quail that had crawled inside. Startled, I failed to shoot. Mack looked at me as if to ask, "Why are you carrying that shotgun?" Once again, I learned: Never try to second-guess a pointer's nose.

How those birds conceived the idea of using the slop jar as a hideaway is beyond me, but in this case, it proved most effective! Perhaps they were members of the aforementioned outdoor-privy covey and, thus, were familiar with slop jars. To recapitulate: In the past forty years quail have changed their habits a great deal. As one old farmer told me, "Burds jes ain't actin' like burds any mo."

Dressin' Quail

Chapter XXII

Early in life, I was introduced to the notion that the only proper way to dress quail is the "pick and singe" method—a procedure of carefully pulling off all the feathers, including those on the wings, without damaging the skin. Then the bird is singed over a flame, preferably using smokeless brown paper, to burn off the pinfeathers. The final step is to cut off the head and feet and remove the viscera through the vent.

Keeping the skin intact allows culinary magic to occur, because the birds don't dry out when cooking. As a matter of fact, genteel people believed so strongly in this manner of dressing quail that doing it otherwise branded your upbringing as severely deficient. Skinning meant, at best, that you were unmannered and, at worst, a barbarian.

I swallowed this dogma hook, line, and sinker, winning nodding approval from my father and Uncle Hal. Consequently, at fifteen minutes per bird, I spent many an hour being most genteel. Then came the time, at age twenty-three, when I faced a pile of at least twenty-five birds to clean. A light (long overdue) went on in my head. I realized that neither my father nor uncle had ever dressed a bird; someone else always did it while they sipped bourbon and waxed eloquently about the excesses of the New Deal.

I tossed the "pick and singe" tradition to the wind and skinned those birds. I've been doing so ever since. I confess to an occasional twinge of remorse, especially when I imagine them looking down at me disapprovingly from above. But the time saved is worth the shame. In a blind taste test, I doubt whether many diners could distinguish skinned from plucked quail. Even if they could, I honestly don't care.

To dress quail, they must be dead. Let's briefly outline how to dispatch wounded quail. Assuming the pointer delivers the bird still alive—in my case a big assumption—it is necessary to end the bird's life quickly. Certainly it is poor form to have a stunned quail suddenly wake up and fly out of the game bag, especially in one's kitchen. I have seen multiple techniques used to effect this conclusion, ranging from whacking the bird's head on the shotgun stock, to pulling the head off and feeding it to the dog as a reward. To each his own. My gunstock gets enough trauma while hunting without using it as an anvil. Also, my dogs don't need any encouragement to eat birds. Two techniques work well: Break the neck where it joins the body, or use the thumb to break the backbone at the juncture of the chest and abdomen.

Skinning requires about fifteen seconds per bird—a sixty-fold reduction in time. To dress quail by skinning, all that is needed is a sharp pair of small scissors capable of cutting the bones. I have found that large kitchen shears or poultry shears are too cumbersome. A sharp knife is adequate also.

Cut off the feet first, then the neck and wings where they join the body. Beginning in the front, pull the skin off the bird except for the tail feathers. (Sometimes a few extra seconds are needed on the back near the tail.) The tail is cut off and the point of the scissors inserted in the hole where the tail was removed; then, cut up the middle of the back and remove the viscera.

Cutting the back facilitates spreading the bird during cooking. If it has been badly shot up or chewed by the dog (a common feature of my peerless retrievers), the damaged meat can be trimmed with scissors. This method also facilitates the removal of shot, perhaps saving the cost of expensive dental work.

Some people want only the breasts, which simplifies the procedure even more. After removing the head and wings, the breast is skinned and cut away from the rest. I use this technique in dressing doves, but not quail; quail leg meat is excellent.

Lastly, wash gently with cold water and either cook or refrigerate. If you are going to freeze the birds, make sure they are tightly enclosed in Saran Wrap, then wrapped in either aluminum foil or freezer paper, dated, and placed in a Zip-Lock bag.

Packages tend to get lost in a freezer. I have had birds that were frozen for ten years, but when properly packaged, the taste was acceptable. Improperly wrapped, they'll develop freezer burn and become ruined in short order.

Mostly I hunt in hot-weather country, and to avoid spoilage, birds are cleaned as soon as possible after the hunt is over. However, even this procedure is not enough for a friend of mine. After a successful shot, he immediately dresses the bird in the field, using his pocketknife to slit the vent and then digs in with his fingers to pull out the entrails. I don't know whether this quick-as-possible approach reduces spoilage, but it certainly produces filthy fingers.

Conversely, I haven't tried the European method of hanging birds until they rot sufficiently for the tail to fall off, so I won't comment, except to say that it seems disgusting.

If memory serves me correctly, I was first introduced to the "pick-and-singe" technique of dressing birds at a very early age. This episode taught me a number of important lessons. On my sixth birthday, I received a Daisy air rifle. My father instructed me regarding the safe use, as well as the appropriate targets, for my new BB gun. Bluejays and English sparrows, considered vermin, were acceptable quarry. All songbirds as well as the neighbor's cat were off limits.

After several months of practice, I became reasonably proficient and had pretty much eliminated the English sparrows from our environs. One day in the early spring, we were inundated with migratory robins. I became suddenly possessed by a devilish meanness, and I killed seven or eight of these birds. As if by magic, my father immediately became aware of my misdeed. After a significant and painful spanking and being informed that my precious BB gun was to be impounded for six months, he decided that additional punishment should be meted out.

I was made to dress the birds (pick-and-singe). My mother would cook them, and I would eat them for supper. This punishment was devised for me to understand that anything (except vermin) that I killed should be eaten. I'm certain that he thought that the awful taste would forever fix in my mind the gravity of my misdeed.

At any rate, my mother reluctantly cooked the robins—country fried with plenty of gravy. (Meat prepared by my mother was usually over-cooked and closely resembled a cinder, but her gravy was absolutely delicious.)

That evening, dinner was served. I took my seat rather gingerly (my rear-end was still sore), and I prepared for a horrible culinary experience. My father glared at me from across the table. Anticipating the worst, I choked down the first bird. Guess what? It was delicious. I quickly consumed three more, along with gravy and rice. At this juncture, my father, realizing that something was amiss, tasted one of the other birds and broke out laughing. His plan to punish me by making me devour an awful-tasting critter had failed completely. I quickly finished the remaining robins and could have eaten more.

In spite of the failed punishment, I got the message. When six months elapsed and I was allowed to resume shooting the BB gun, I never killed another songbird. I do continue to wonder whether robins are truly as good to eat as I remember?

To return to the primary topic of preparing quail for the table, the secret to cooking quail is not to overcook. When frying, lightly flour and cook for five minutes at high temperature; even if the bones are slightly red, the meat will be moist and delicious.

There are countless recipes for preparing quail. Most involve smothering the taste of the birds in mixtures of wine, herbs, butter, garlic, sugar, and spices. Often these produce reasonably good fare, but the results don't taste like quail. In fact, with enough of these ingredients, shoe leather can be turned into a gourmet dish. At any rate, a dish of good-tasting, fried quail does not require the waste of time necessary to "pick-and-singe."

Covey Call

Chapter XXIII

The popular name for the eastern subspecies of quail is derived from its characteristic call: "bob . . . white." This cheery salutation, heard only during the breeding season, late spring and early summer, is given by the male either seeking companionship or as a territorial warning. For the rest of the year, the most characteristic sound made by bobwhite quail is the covey call, which is a low-pitched single or double note having a rising inflection and used primarily to bring together scattered members of the covey. A similar call may also be heard early in the morning before the quail leave the roost. Unfortunately, predators have been known to either mimic or at least utilize their knowledge of the covey call to find quail.

This story relates an unusual experience that I had while bird hunting and features the covey call. To set the stage, the time was the early 1980s. Much of the farmland near my home in the Piedmont region of North Carolina had been taken out of cultivation. Tobacco farming essentially ceased, and some of the residual land was planted in corn, soybeans, and small grains. The fallow land became covered with second-growth pines and honeysuckle thickets. Because many of the farms had been abandoned for a long time, it was not unusual to find remnants of deserted homes or barns. There was the ever-present danger of a bird dog falling into an uncovered well or being injured by rusting barbed wire or metal. In general, I avoided these sites. However, these ruins document how the land had been used previously. For example, in late February, I found an old chimney surrounded by nearly an acre of daffodils in full bloom; the former occupants must have loved flowers.

The day in question was in middle January, after the deer season ended, and I had the woods pretty much to myself. The weather was ideal for hunting; it was overcast with little wind blowing and the temperature was about 45 degrees, conditions in which quail frequently feed most of the day.

I hunted on a farm about twenty miles north of Durham, close to the Flat River. The land was primarily covered in woods but did contain several fields of soybeans, which for some reason had not been harvested. I had hunted in this area once before, earlier in the season, but without any luck.

Tiny, a four-year-old effervescent and energetic pointer, Pepper, a hardheaded but effective setter, and I began our outing around 2:00 P.M. After convincing Pepper that he needed to hunt with me today, rather than off on his own (setters are like that), I walked toward the cultivated land. About 2:30 P.M., I found the dogs pointing in the middle of a field of soybeans. A covey of about twelve birds flushed and flew toward a densely covered area at the edge of the field. The birds appeared not to scatter widely, and I anticipated some good single-bird shooting. I shot one bird on the covey rise, which was only winged. The bird ran into a small windrow with both Pepper and Tiny in hot pursuit. After about five minutes, Tiny appeared with a thoroughly dead bird in her mouth (Tiny was very effective but not a tender-mouthed retriever).

I began walking toward the thicket where the covey had disappeared. When I was within fifty yards or so of the edge of the field, I heard a distinct covey call. (It is highly unusual for quail to start calling immediately after being flushed; they usually wait several hours and generally call only in the late afternoon.) I entered the thicket. Pepper and Tiny were about fifty yards to my right. After walking about twenty to thirty yards, I suddenly became aware that I was in an old family cemetery.

The cemetery had obviously been untouched for a number of years and was overgrown with small trees and underbrush. The copings on the perimeter walls had all but disappeared, and a few of the gravestones were turned over. However, on one marble stone, with the top broken and the name unreadable, I was able to decipher the letters CSA, followed by the date, May 1864. After staring at the marker for several minutes, I suddenly realized the significance.

During that terrible month, thousands of soldiers—both Confederate and Union—were killed as the two armies commanded by Generals Lee and Grant fought multiple battles from Spotsylvania to Cold Harbor in northern Virginia. In fact, my maternal great-grandfather, who was a surgeon under General Longstreet, had written a letter to his father (which I have) describing the horrible carnage. Obviously, the man buried under this marker died while fighting for the Confederacy.

These thoughts or daydreams completely occupied my mind. A slight noise behind me brought me back to reality. I looked around. Pepper and Tiny were pointing toward me, both having a quizzical look, as if to ask why I was standing there, rather than walking up the birds. I took one step forward. What seemed like the entire covey flushed again and flew toward the dense low grounds near the river. I had been so preoccupied with my thoughts that I failed to shoot. I continued to think about the War Between the States, the soldier, and the quail.

On the other side of the grave, I found a honeysuckle thicket nearly filled with roosts. Obviously, these quail used the old gravesite frequently.

Tiny, Pepper, and I started hunting toward the river. After walking about one hundred yards, I again heard a distinct covey call behind me. I retraced my steps thinking that there must be a single bird at the gravesite that hadn't flushed. We hunted the entire area thoroughly, but to no avail. Where did the covey call come from?

I decided not to pursue the singles further and hunted in several other soybean fields. As I remember, we found two more coveys, killed three or four quail, and had an excellent time.

About 5:00 P.M., we retraced our steps toward the truck and came to the same field. As I passed the gravesite, I heard a low-pitched covey call. It was getting quite late, and the shadows of the evening made the edge of the field indistinct. In my mind's eye I could see, shrouded in the evening mist, a Confederate soldier dressed in gray homespun, carrying his musket into battle and dying for "The Lost Cause."

A bullet at the Bloody Angle
Ended the War for me.
On this red clay hillside,
I rest for eternity.

Though the solace of silence surrounds me
Unbroken by earthly din,
Through the cheerful call of the covey,
I come back to the home of men.

The birds probably were near the grave and could be flushed again. I decided to leave them alone. Perhaps the soldier in the abandoned grave enjoyed the companionship of quail. Who was I to deprive him of his friends?

I returned home. I hunted on the farm only once more during that season and found this covey. I didn't shoot. When the birds flushed, I heard a soft, but distinct, covey call. I have relived this experience many times.

Bird Hunting: Is There a Future?

Chapter XXIV

As with any controversial issue, opinions on the future of sport hunting divide the citizenry into three groups: 1) Proponent—well-informed conservationists, hunters, farmers, or other outdoor people; 2) Opponent—extreme environmentalists, animal "cultists," and general "do-gooders"; and 3) Ambivalent—the large uncommitted majority who lean either toward the antihunting camp or have not given significant thought to the subject. Obviously, this latter group holds the key to the future. Convincing this majority to support hunting is essential, but it will not be easy.

Consider the following: Most people born in this country after World War II grew up in an urban environment in which there were no opportunities to experience sport hunting. They have been influenced to dislike hunting and the associated killing of animals by negative grade-school curricula, a generally hostile media, and a gaggle of obsessed, misinformed "animal alarmists." Not that they mind eating pork, steak, or chicken—meat that comes from the supermarket that someone else slaughters. The fact that hunting involves the death of animals and usually is associated with blood is especially negative; hence, the derogatory term "blood sport."

As a rule, people abhor the sight of blood, at least, where killing animals is concerned. The sanguineous slaughter of their fellow citizens in a television, video, or movie spectacular is quite a different matter! At any rate, "killing-for-sport" has been depicted as an atavistic urge that should have died with the demise of the cave man. Remember, however, that citizens exposed to these views constitute a large majority of the voting public and control the ballot box. Unfortunately, at this time in America, a simple majority—not inalienable rights—dictate the laws.

What then, if anything, may hunters or similarly minded people do to preserve their sport? Obviously, the secret lies in educating the general public as to the very positive aspects of hunting. Many organizations, such as the National Rifle Association, United Sportsman of America, and Safari Club

International, are making valiant efforts in this regard. Their work should be enthusiastically supported. Hunters interested in the long-term viability of their sport must be willing to spend time and money in a crusade to educate the general public. Any forum available should be used, from one-on-one conversations to group gatherings.

The positive features of hunting may be categorized into three general components: Conservation, economic, and individual gratification. Conservation of land and animal resources is of major concern to most people. In spite of misinformation to the contrary, habitat destruction and urban sprawl—not hunting—has been the prime cause of wildlife disappearance. In fact, the successful conservation of many wildlife species owes its genesis to hunters. For example, Teddy Roosevelt, the father of conservation in this country, was a dedicated hunter. He led the battle to set aside large tracks of land, such as Yellowstone Park, to maintain adequate habitat for many animal species, both game and otherwise. The enormous success of conservation in the United States has been made possible both by the efforts and the financial resources of hunters. The large sums of money generated from hunting licenses and taxes on sporting equipment, (e.g., Pittman-Robertson Act), plus the many gifts from hunters to organizations such as Ducks Unlimited, have been the primary support for preservation of wildlife.

As a purely economic factor, hunting provides a multibillion-dollar source of revenue, especially in many of our western states. In fact, the importance of hunting game animals as a source of revenue ranks at the top in many African countries as well. The concept of game animals as a renewable financial resource has been widely accepted by most wildlife biologists.

Conservation and economics would seem an easy sell to most people if the data are presented in a dispassionate way, but frequently it is not. Logic or facts may not always carry the day with many of the misguided public. "If it weren't for hunters like you" the uninformed may quip, "there would be no need for conservation. All animals would be plentiful." The fact that this attitude remains after a clear presentation of the positive components of hunting is difficult to swallow. However, getting mad and giving up won't help.

A fortuitous and unexpected reason to support hunting by suburban dwellers has been the recent explosion in the deer population. Deer are everywhere, causing serious automobile accidents and voraciously destroying vegetable gardens, ornamental plants, and shrubbery around homes. These problems have led many nonhunters to reconsider the idealic picture of Bambi and lean toward supporting hunting as a measure to control the deer population. In some areas, nonmigratory Canadian geese are causing similar problems.

The third category, the all-encompassing contentment derived from hunting, is difficult to explain to the uninitiated. An example from my own experience illustrates the point. Several years ago, Joey O'Bannon wanted to record some bird-hunting sequences to use as a promotional guide for his hunting preserve. We spent the better part of a day and a half in an ideal scenic location filming spectacular dog work and, frankly, reasonably good shooting on my part.

The video tape had it all: The dogs pointing, backing, handling running quail requiring multiple relocations, several breathtaking covey rises, and good retrieving, including a segment of a dog catching a wounded quail. We had captured much of the essence of quail hunting.

Extremely proud of this production, I showed the tape to several of my friends—people who by no means were antihunting. They watched for about five minutes, grew restless, and finally one of them said the magic words, "I really feel sorry for those birds being killed." This response stunned me! My friends were completely oblivious to the spectacular hunting sequences unfolding before their very eyes. I naively believed that anyone witnessing this spectacle would wish to participate in the excitement derived from quail hunting.

If the apathetic public is a difficult sell, where should the education effort be concentrated? By far the best hope to preserve hunting is to make a major effort to initiate young people into the sport. "If you catch a Scotsman early enough," Dr. Johnson once remarked, "you can do something with him." I truly believe that unless conditioned otherwise, a young, open mind will thrill to the sight of a pair of pointers performing flawlessly or feel the excitement of being scared out of half their wits by a covey rise.

When I was ten years old, this experience caused an indelible positive influence on me; in fact, that is why I hunt. I'm sure waterfowl and big-game hunters feel the same way about their hunting sports.

One extremely important task for sportsman-hunters interested in the future is to clean up their own act. Nothing could be more devastating to the reputation of hunting than the behavior of a few "slobs." Trespassing, destroying property, loud and boisterous behavior, especially when drinking, are all actions that have painted hunters with a bad brush in the eyes of many people. The hunting fraternity must do its best to eliminate this element.

Hunters must stick together and not allow any encroachment of their sport to occur. The total abolition of hunting will not occur in one fell swoop, but more gradually, in a series of prohibitory laws. Bird hunters must not sit idly by while big-game hunting is curtailed; they will be next. As Ben Franklin said, "We must hang together, or surely we will hang separately."

One thing hunters must not do is to underestimate the power and dedication of the antihunting groups. The truly dedicated animal "cultist" or "terrorist" (both words are applicable) should be considered a menace. These people will use whatever tactics, legal or otherwise, necessary to prevent hunting. Witness the unlawful harassment of sport hunters, which is now common practice.

Another approach by the antihunting forces is to employ the legal processes, such as environmental impact statements and ballot-box initiatives to restrict hunting. The vote in California that outlawed mountain lion hunting, for example, has all but signed the death warrant for the Rocky Mountain big-horned sheep, due to the increase of the mountain lion population. In addition, the number of attacks on humans by mountain lions has increased significantly. This initiative uniformly was opposed by the knowledgeable game management authorities! Do the antihunting forces really care? No! According to them, the killing of animals by man is the only problem, and it must be stopped—no matter the consequences.

How to deal with animal cultists? Don't back down! One problem with most hunters is that they are generally nice people who do not thrive on confrontation. This attitude is not going to work when trying to educate the public regarding hunting.

The extreme position espoused by the most vociferous antihunters must be clearly illustrated. For example, members of PETA believe any animal from shrew to man is of equal importance in the cosmic scheme of things and should be accorded similar "rights." The disciples of this creed like to brag that they don't eat meat or wear animal products. Thus, they are on the side of the "angels" and better than the rest of us. Not so! The vegetables they eat and the cotton they wear are grown on tilled land. In order to produce these items, the habitat for wildlife has been markedly degraded by cultivation and the animals occupying the land either dispersed or killed.

It should be made clear that the only way not to kill any animal life, while providing food and fiber for man, would be for all of us to eat rocks and go naked! This argument will place these twits in an untenable position and will help to convince the general public not to listen to their crackpot ideas.

In summary, in spite of the long odds, hunters must continue to "fight the good fight" to preserve the sport and, while it is available, enjoy the totality of the hunting experience—being close to God in the great outdoors. Perhaps we live at the "tail end" of a tradition stretching back to the time when our forefathers first crawled out of the primordial slime. If sport hunting disappears; God forbid, man and beast alike will be by far the poorer.

Will I Keep on Hunting?

Chapter XXV

The fact is, most quail hunters do not pursue a lifelong immersion in this sport, and the question is, why do they quit? Will I be similarly affected? As detailed previously in the chapter "Why Hunt Birds," there are a variety of sportsmen who hunt quail. Certainly, the majority of hunters participating in this sport are not seriously committed to it. The reasons for this "some-timey" approach to quail hunting by these nimrods is not germane to this argument.

I am examining the question of "Why do dyed-in-the-wool, avid, true, dedicated quail hunters stop?" There are a number of situations that logically might seem to bear on their decision to give up. As examples: 1) They moved for business or other reasons and now are living in an area where quail hunting isn't possible. 2) A health problem made walking laborious. 3) They married a disciple of PETA who violently objects to hunting. These and multiple other situations would seem sufficient to curtail hunting. However, true bird hunters would find a way to hunt, in spite of all these obstacles.

There is only one explanation for quitting that is consistently espoused by former avid quail hunters: A dog with which they have hunted for a number of years died. With their companion's death, the fun of quail hunting disappeared. I can fully understand this feeling. I have had it myself on a number of occasions. Undoubtedly, all of the situations listed above, including a militant wife, would not stop them from quail hunting if this dog were still alive.

The only remedy is to find another dog. The problem is somewhat alleviated if the hunter has two to three dogs of different ages, so as one grows older, others are available. However, a truly irreplaceable dog is, by definition, irreplaceable. An often-repeated truism says that in one's lifetime you should consider yourself very blessed if you find one good dog and one good woman. I won't comment on the latter part of this maxim, but certainly good dogs are very few and very far between. At any rate, there is no therapy for the loss of an outstanding bird dog—except to get another one.

Will I quit? I've very nearly done it many times in the past. Always, I was able to find another dog, perhaps not truly a brag dog, but good enough for me. I hope I can continue to be so lucky.

It's Over

For fifty years, we've hunted quail—
Those pointer dogs and me.
Many an hour we spent afield,
On a quest for another covey.
But every time when a dog grew old
And I saw his work was done,
An empty heart cried out, Enough!
Please quit! Hang up your gun.
It's hard to bid a final good-bye
To a true and cherished friend.
From Spot to Hannah and all between,
I've cried when their day did end.
But always before, a younger dog
Arose to stave off the night.
Though I missed the ones that went before,
I continued to hunt Bobwhite.
Now Faith is old and slowing down.
I'm sure she'll be the last.
The final chapter; this is the end.
My hunting days have past.
But wait! A litter of pointer pups
Are growing up in the pen.
I wonder: Will there be another
To make me hunt again?
(1998)

A Quail Hunter's "Must Have" Excuses

Chapter XXVI

An adept quail hunter must be reasonably proficient in a variety of situations. One of the most important is to be facile at constructing a series of well-thought-out reasons or excuses to explain apparent missteps. Two important, and in the main, unrelated situations come to mind: 1) missing quail and 2) spending excessive money on pointers and/or high-grade double-barrel shotguns. The following will codify my current thoughts regarding these two issues.

One component, large or small depending on the individual's point of view, of successful quail hunting is to bag the quarry with a reasonable degree of consistency. Even in my best years, I was never a particularly good performer in this regard, but remained egotistical enough to search for reasons or excuses for my poor marksmanship. Over a lifetime of mediocre shooting, I have developed an impressive list of both reasons and excuses for missing. This list has become extensive enough so that I cannot instantly recall all of its contents and apply the appropriate alibi. In order to alleviate this situation, I set about the task of codifying and characterizing each reason or excuse so that recalling them when needed will be made much easier.

This endeavor was stimulated by a story I heard several years ago describing an episode that occurred in a long-term prison. A visitor was being shown around while the prisoners were locked in their cells. All of a sudden, someone cried out in a loud voice "Twenty-three." The prisoners erupted in laughter for about three or four minutes and then calmed down. A few minutes later, someone yelled out "Forty-four," and raucous laughter ensued. After this scenario was repeated several times, only with different numbers, the visitor asked the guard, "What was going on"?

The guard answered, "Well, the prisoners have all been here for a long time. They've heard the same jokes over and over again and decided to give each joke a number. So, rather than tell the joke, any resident can yell out the number and everyone becomes amused and laughs. This technique works quite well."

After some thought, I decided to implement a similar approach to express both the reasons and excuses for missing quail. After missing and uttering two or three choice cuss words (so that the dogs fully appreciate the fact that I have failed to hold up my end of the bargain), I can simply shout out the appropriate number. Thus, I save myself the effort of articulating a specific explanation. Obviously, for this approach to be effective for other individuals involved in the hunt, they must be conversant with my system. However, since I usually hunt by myself, and only have to convince myself which reason or excuse is paramount, I have found that this plan is quite functional.

In the following, I have attempted to classify the multiple reasons and excuses for missing quail. In putting together this list, I have included both situations: Either I failed to shoot, or I shot, but missed. Although it would seem that these problems are quite different, the causes are similar. It's of little practical value to try to separate them.

The first group (A) includes what I believe are truly valid reasons for my ineptitude. The second group (B) contains questionable excuses. The third group (C) describes excuses that are so ridiculous that even I do not believe them!

Group A

1) I was so enthralled by the pointers' performance—pointing and backing—that I forgot to shoot until the birds were out of range. Although this may sound like so much crap to the uninitiated, at least from my perspective, this is the most valid reason in this entire epistle.

2) The bird flew directly into the sun and I was temporarily blinded. (This is not a good reason to use on an overcast day.)

3) The bird flew toward the swamp buggy. I did not shoot for fear of having to buy another radiator. One is enough!

4) The bird flew very low above the ground and I was worried about inadvertently shooting a dog. This is valid only when shooting at a bird that does not flush with the covey rise. Otherwise, the dog should be behind the shooter and not in the line of fire.

5) The gun was breached to reload; thus, I couldn't put a shell in the chamber and close it fast enough to shoot. Actually, this is a reasonably common occurrence when shooting singles that flush at random intervals. After I shoot at one bird, I invariably open the gun, eject the cartridge, and reload, even if

a live round is still in the other barrel. The utility of this strategy is somewhat questionable, but it does provide a semivalid reason for failing to fire.

6) It was too dark for me to see the bird well. Shooting at a "sundown covey" once was great fun—no longer. As the surroundings darken, I might as well save the ammunition.

7) The bird flew behind a bush or tree just as I was about to shoot. In my earlier years, I developed the "Greenfield Shuffle," which allowed me to move rapidly to change my position and complete the shot. Of late, my feet seem fixed in concrete. The "Greenfield Shuffle" is a thing of the past.

8) While walking to the pointing dogs, I got tangled up in a palmetto root and fell. As I flopped to the ground, the first order of business was to protect my precious double-barrel shotgun. As a consequence, my knee hit the ground sideways—a direction that it is not constructed to bend. Thank goodness, the shotgun was not harmed, but I could not stand up.

Group B

1) The stock of the shotgun got caught in my clothes and, thus, could not be mounted properly. If one practices mounting the shotgun in the appropriate manner, baggy clothes won't get in the way.

2) The safety could not be released. In fact, a safety may "freeze up" if one is too sorry to clean and oil the gun properly.

3) The shotgun malfunctioned and failed to fire. This is only valid if one is hunting with an automatic, a pump, or a cheap double barrel. This will not occur when using a high-grade double shotgun.

4) The gun doesn't fit properly, thus resulting in shooting either under or over the flying quail. This certainly may be an issue if one is using a borrowed gun. However, it should be dealt with prior to beginning the hunt. Familiarity with one's shotgun is an essential feature of reasonable quail hunting.

5) The ammunition either did not pattern appropriately or was insufficiently powerful to incapacitate the quail. This is only valid if one chooses the cheapest ammunition available or selects the wrong shot size. If the hunter doesn't buy either #7½ or #8 shot, or can't afford a reasonably high-quality shotgun shell, he should watch TV and not go quail hunting.

6) So many birds flushed that I could not pick one out. The likelihood that this will occur in modern-day quail hunting is remote at best.

Group C

1) The flushed bird resembled either a "stink" bird or a snipe, but not a quail. If the hunter can't identify a quail, either he should buy glasses or try another sport.

2) The quail, obviously dead, flew on with his "heart shot out." An alternative is that an antihunting group issued flak jackets to the quail. Actually, I like both of these fanciful excuses.

3) Just as I was about to shoot, the dog relieved himself on my leg. Since this behavior occurs only after I miss and the dog is making clear his disgruntlement, it is not a valid excuse for missing.

4) I was certain I heard a rattlesnake sound off and was trying to locate the snake just as the covey flushed. One can expand on this distraction by blaming being charged by a wild hog, a feral bull, or another similar critter. (Implicating lions, tigers, and bears is outside the pale of reality.)

5) Finally, the most unlikely of all: Recently, I read an advertisement by PETA. Momentarily, I was overcome by their screed regarding the ethics of hunting. (In my case, this feeling lasted only a nanosecond and will never be repeated.)

Well, this is, at least, a partial list of reasons and excuses for failure to connect with departing quail. Now the issue to be dealt with is what to do about the situation. Cursing to let the dogs know you have missed and then continuing with the hunt is by far the best course of action. However, one other option is available. Pretend that you did kill a quail, loudly shout "dead bird," and make the dogs come in and begin a fruitless search. After a few minutes of no results, proclaim that the bird ran off into wiregrass, went into a hole, or otherwise disappeared so that the dog cannot locate them. If one wants to get really creative, one might even postulate that the bird stuck his head in his rear-end so far that only a tiny round membrane is left, making it impossible for the dog to find the remains.

Another great excuse is to say that the bird "disappeared" behind an obstruction at the exact moment of the shot and "might" have been killed. While this approach might even fool yourself occasionally, it should not be tried too frequently. Pointers, who despise retrieving anyway, if called upon to carry out many fruitless searches will invariably decide to leave the environs and hunt in another county. (Really, I don't blame them.)

I'm not at all certain if the foregoing has been worth my effort. But, it does provide, at least, a cursory examination of reasons and excuses for coming home empty-handed. Since the list is quite extensive, memorizing the entire group by number might be too difficult a task. Perhaps the best practical approach would be to simply shout out "A," "B," or "C," which would best characterize, in a general fashion, the current situation.

In addition to cataloging the reasons or excuses for missing quail, the "dyed-in-the-wool" bird hunter needs to develop a strategy to justify the expenses involved with pursuing his sport. The two components requiring the greatest expense are the costs of acquiring well-trained bird dogs and, assuming one is so inclined, purchasing high-grade, double-barrel shotguns. The obvious question regarding cost justification is "Justified to whom?" I will not elaborate on this question—preferring to let each individual hunter answer, based on his own circumstances. At any rate, let us deal with the cost of bird dogs first.

There is little to be gained from pining for those halcyon days when a superbly trained pointer could be purchased for $100. It ain't never gonna happen again. Somewhere between $1,500 and $3,000 is the current necessary outlay. In fact, this amount may not guarantee that one is purchasing a good performer. However, for the purposes of this presentation, let us assume that one is lucky and obtains an excellent bird dog for $3,000. That's a lot of money when examined through the lens that an equal amount will heat and cool one's home for at least two years.

My approach is to adopt the "use-cost" strategy. Here's how the "use cost" is figured for this hypothetical situation. The bird dog is currently four years old and will be hunted at least for six years. On the average, I hunt approximately fifty days per year. Exercising grammar-school mathematics (I forgot—this level of computation now is reserved for high school seniors!), one can calculate the cost at $10 a hunt, which is truly a modest price to pay for the companionship of a peerless bird dog. For comparison, it's about the same as the cost of going to a Hollywood movie and being indoctrinated into the wonders of the current liberal agenda. Admittedly, my approach totally ignores the upkeep of the dog, but so what? Conclusion: Three thousand dollars to purchase an excellent bird dog is a very reasonable outlay.

The second area that needs to be justified concerns the outlay required to obtain a fine, double-barrel shotgun. At least in my opinion, bird hunting without such a firearm is a travesty. To advance the argument, let us assume that one obtains a second-hand Purdey shotgun in reasonable condition for $10,000. Actually, the cost is considerably more, but for this discussion, let us assume that one was lucky enough to use the tried-and-true technique of obtaining a fine firearm cheaply, i.e., a divorce requiring instant cash. At any rate, this high-quality, double-barrel shotgun will be employed on all future hunts.

As before, I will utilize the "use-cost" strategy with one very different wrinkle. Again, let us assume that the shotgun will be used fifty days a year for a twenty-year period or the same $10 a hunt. However, let us not forget one very important item. Twenty years from now, if cared for appropriately, the shotgun will double in value and be worth $20,000. Thus, rather than an outlay of $10 a hunt, one is actually making $10 a hunt. Again, the cost of ammunition and other trivial items are ignored in the calculation, but the logic is still impeccable. The conclusion seems inescapable: Purchase a very expensive double-barrel shotgun and pay the entire costs of one's bird hunting. Even better, the more expensive the initial outlay, the more the quail hunter is pocketing with every hunt.

While there are probably a number of other reasons or excuses quail hunters will need to employ to justify their avocation, those described should be a good beginning. At least they can serve as a guide for future similar machinations.

What's in a Name?

Chapter XXVII

To paraphrase/mangle a famous passage from Shakespeare, "a pointer by any other name would smell as sweet/sour." (The definition of sweet/sour depends on one's own perception of the smell emanating from a wet dog.) At any rate, this epistle attempts to address the question of "How critical is the choice of a name for a pointer?" Does the name in any way influence the dog's hunting capabilities? Since my dogs respond adequately only to a loud and forceful expostulation of "son-of-a-bitch," it would be perfectly reasonable to end this quest for an appropriate name and rely solely on this moniker.

However, I will ignore this impeccable logic and proceed to develop a better and more varied strategy for naming the pointer. First, let's confine this search to finding a label by which the dog can be taught to respond. The use of multi-word names that are used to register the dog, such as Sergeant's Super Selection or Rambling Rose's Revelation, will not be addressed further. Also, I will not address the techniques of spelling the owner's name backward to identify a certain family of dogs (employed in the naming of the Elhew strain). What I am searching for is a strategy to come up with an appropriate useful handle, usually referred to as the kennel name.

It seems axiomatic that success in training and hunting a pointer would be facilitated if the dog's attention could be gotten readily—in short, responding to his name. Since the goal is to be certain that the dog recognizes his name, it is clearly better to have a short, characteristic name that can be used to preface simple commands such as "Whoa" or "Come here." Thus, multi-syllable names, no matter how descriptive or unique, generally should be avoided; for example, Wilhelmina, Eucalyptus, or Asphidity are not acceptable. (On the other hand, if these names are chosen, the kennel name could be shortened to Will, Eu, or Ass.)

So far, what has been established is that a relatively short, single-syllable name is preferable. Remember now, we are trying to define an appropriate handle to be attached to a young dog or puppy. From the foregoing, it would seem that the simplest thing to do would be to use common, single-syllable names such as Joe, Tom, Bill, etc. Certainly, this is an acceptable approach, although it does not lend any uniqueness or class to your trusted compatriot. At least in my opinion, the dog deserves a more thoughtful approach in the naming process.

In choosing an appropriate name, one is commonly dealing with the need to name several puppies from a given litter. One approach that I have used in the past with mixed success is to develop a theme. For example, relying on the New Testament, I named three female puppies Faith, Hope, and Charity. Faith turned out to be an outstanding, if a somewhat obnoxious, bird-finding machine. Hope and Charity died early, one from ingesting rat poison and the other from a rattlesnake bite, which proves, I guess, that biblical names don't necessarily protect the animal from mishaps. Also, I designated Matthew, Mark, Luke, and John, but unfortunately, only Luke turned out to be a keeper.

One approach that I would strongly advise against is using the name of a dog owned in the past that was judged to be outstanding. It is highly unlikely that the puppy will ever measure up in the owner's mind to this prior paragon. Hence, the name should die with the dog. My first, and certainly one of my best bird dogs, was named Spot. Not a very impressive name but descriptive, since he had one large liver spot on his right side.

At any rate, the previously mentioned Faith had one of the sorriest litters that I ever raised. It never occurred to me at the time of the naming process that her progeny would be anything but outstanding dogs. So, I gave many of them the name of a dog that I had owned in the past. The puppy I named Spot did resemble his predecessor in coloration, but in nothing else. A sorrier specimen of a pointer bird dog would be hard to imagine. When I quit trying to train him to hunt birds, he even flunked out as a hog dog. At any rate, I spent far too much time on this worthless specimen simply because I had named him for my first pointer. Unfortunately, the rest of Faith's litter, all named for previous standouts, turned out to be, at best, mediocre. To recapitulate, if you own a good dog, let the name die with that dog.

Although it would seem obvious, another group of names to be ruled out would be specific cuss words or other unacceptable names that are inappropriate to shout in polite company. (It's probably unnecessary to give multiple examples of these verboten names.)

The names chosen for my best litter came from Shakespearian characters. In so doing, I broke my short-name rule. To that end, Hamlet, Horatio, Humphrey, and Hal, along with sisters Cordelia, Miranda, Kate, and Portia, were christened. An additional "method in my madness" was related to the fact that Joey O'Bannon, my hunting companion and partner in bird-dog adventures for nearly twenty-five years, agreed to use my choices. Hearing his south-Florida, cracker accent admonishing Horatio . . . Ho-ra-ti-o . . . for some malfeasance was enough to make me laugh to the point of becoming faint. Ulysses, Scylla, and Charybdis, named for characters in Homer's *Odyssey* evoked a similar response. An even more daunting task for Joey came when I named ten puppies for the brightest stars—Betelgeuse, Arcturus, Procyon, Rigel, Deneb, Antares, Altair, Sirius, Vega, and Capella. (I really have a perverted sense of humor!)

I agree that one-syllable names are the easiest for the dog to learn. However, giving the dog a distinctive name also is an important goal, so the moniker may require two or more syllables. Multi-syllable names can be shortened if necessary. For example, the aforementioned Charybdis, which is a unique and very classy name, currently is identified as Rib.

Although it may seem obvious, my advice is to stick with the dog's name once it is chosen. One cannot expect a dog to respond to several different names or variations of the same name. Especially avoid using one name in praising the dog and another when admonishing him.

Perhaps this entire exercise has been "much ado about nothing"; however, I don't think so. My own feeling is that each young dog should be given a unique and well-thought-out name. Frankly, I believe a dog named Ulysses is much more likely to develop into a high-class bird dog than one that will go through life burdened by a common name like Bud. So, what's in a name? Put yourself in the dog's position and try to come up with a name that both you and the dog can be justly proud.

Troubles with Snakes

Chapter XXVIII

While describing the various aspects of quail hunting to the uninitiated, I am frequently asked, "Aren't you afraid of being bitten by a poisonous snake?" The definitive answer is "No." I have, however, experienced a few unwanted episodes with these reptiles over a sixty-year time span, episodes that probably should be penned for posterity.

My first encounter with a serpent, at age five or six, involved being bitten by a water snake. I was walking near the edge of a small creek, approximately thirty miles south of Atlanta, on a farm that belonged to my family. To say the least, the farm was run down, and much of it was overgrown with "bugger bushes." The occupants at the time were several families of tenant farmers who had planted an acre or two of cotton and had done little else. In the past, the acreage had been a well-kept plantation, but by the time of my first snake encounter, the main house was no longer standing, having suffered the consequences of Sherman's invading hoards, and only a few dilapidated shacks remained. At any rate, my parents occasionally visited this shabby venue, where they would eat a picnic lunch while reminiscing about better times.

As I walked along the streambed, I stepped on a large brown snake that immediately turned and bit me on the right ankle. Scared to death, I screamed for my father. The snake disappeared. I was hustled off to a local physician. My father and mother were quite certain that I had been bitten by a cottonmouth moccasin and soon would be quite ill. Although there were no definite fang marks, only scratches, the physician decorated my ankle with two reasonably large crosses, causing profuse bleeding and little else. (The scars are still evident seventy years later.)

Other than the problems associated with being frightened, primarily by my parents, and bleeding from the iatrogenic cuts, there were no other untoward results. Undoubtedly, I had been over-treated for the bite of a harmless water snake. Interestingly enough, rather than evoking a lifelong fear of snakes, I actually went the other way—probably becoming too cavalier regarding the dangers of poisonous reptiles.

The environs around Atlanta where I hunted rabbits with beagles were occupied by only one variety of poisonous snake, the copperhead. Although I ran the dogs in the summertime when the snakes were about, I never experienced or remember ever seeing a snake while so engaged, nor were any of my dogs ever bitten. Obviously, the majority of my hunting was done during the cold weather when the snakes are hibernating.

My first real encounter with poisonous snakes occurred when I began hunting near Thomasville, Georgia. Both cottonmouth moccasins and eastern diamondback rattlesnakes were indigenous. The winters in that area were such that a warm spell might occur in early December, January, or February and last for a week or so. The snakes that had been hibernating emerged, and although torpid, were fully capable of inflicting serious bites. I don't remember ever being concerned about this problem, but my Uncle Hal, who paid for the quail lease and with whom I hunted, was deathly afraid of snakes. He would never walk in thick areas where he could not see the ground. Along with the 275 pounds he had to mobilize, having to watch every footstep slowed us down immeasurably.

Actually, I can only remember one incident involving a diamondback rattlesnake. I was hunting alone in a sandy area covered with gallberries. Spot pointed, but his demeanor was quite different. Although pointed, his stance was unusual; he gradually moved backward. At that juncture, I heard the characteristic rattle and quickly dispatched the snake before any harm could be done. Whether Spot had any prior experience with rattlesnakes, I have no idea, but it was quite clear that he recognized something was amiss.

When I discussed this incident with the owner of the farm, he told me that a local veterinarian had related the fact that one of his clients had had two very expensive bird dogs killed recently. Apparently, the dogs had availed themselves of the shade under the porch of an old house during the noon hour and had inadvertently crawled on top of a large rattlesnake. They apparently had no innate fear of snakes and failed to survive the encounter.

Although the area I hunted in middle Georgia did contain cottonmouths and canebrake rattlesnakes, I never saw one. Also, during the entire time I hunted in Piedmont North Carolina, both fox hunting and bird hunting, I never encountered a poisonous reptile.

This long, unbroken happy spell changed when I began hunting in Florida. There are four poisonous snakes that inhabit the environs near where I hunted: eastern diamondback rattlesnake, cottonmouth moccasin, pigmy rattlesnake, and coral snake. The latter is an innocuous reptile, but quite deadly. It is secretive to the point that it is extremely unlikely to be encountered during hunting. However, I once had a frightening experience with a coral snake.

During the first seven or eight years, I hunted at Indiantown with Joey O'Bannon. I bunked in a small aluminum travel trailer (The Silver Bullet). A couple of concrete blocks served as the steps to the trailer. The bathroom facilities were never hooked up, so of necessity, I had to walk to a bathroom in a nearby trailer or alternatively "water" the yard, depending on the circumstances. One night, I opened the trailer door and started to step out onto the concrete blocks. I was barefoot. The moon was out, and I saw something move on the step. I shined the flashlight and illuminated a sixteen-inch coral snake coiled on the step, giving me the once over. Yes, it was a coral snake (red on yellow, kill a fellow) not a milk snake or a scarlet king snake. While attempting to find a cudgel to dispatch the creature, it slithered under the trailer and was no longer visible. Forgetting the "call of nature," I quickly shut the door. After calming down, I finally went to sleep. The next morning, we searched high and low for the intruder, but couldn't find it. To say the least, for the next few days, I was careful about where I walked at night. As a follow-up, Joey killed a coral snake near the trailer a week or so after I left.

During the twenty-year period of Florida hunting, I've only seen one cottonmouth near a drainage ditch. I'm far more concerned about the dangers to the dogs and possibly to myself from a cottonmouth vs. a rattlesnake. The cottonmouth is aggressive and will not try to get away. Also, it does not sound a warning with the telltale rattle. I had one encounter with a cottonmouth while hunting single birds near a canal. The dogs weren't around, and I quickly dispatched the serpent.

Pygmy rattlesnakes are a rarity. I have seen only one, which happened to be crossing the road in the Hobe Sound area, and I spied it from the swamp buggy. The small snake was appropriately squashed by the tire.

However, I have had several unhappy encounters with eastern diamondback rattlesnakes during the past twenty years. Recognizing that I was hunting in areas where snakes were fairly common, I have always carried the appropriate antivenom on the truck along with cortisone and the paraphernalia to lance the skin.

A disquieting incident occurred while hunting in LaBelle. Two pointers were hunting together, one running approximately thirty yards behind the other. (I detest this behavior in bird dogs, but occasionally it happens.) The first dog passed the snake and obviously agitated it. When the second dog, Lib, ran close to it, the coiled snake struck. She was bitten in the back leg on the muscle. Obviously in pain, she ran to the truck. After dealing with the offending serpent, I found one fang hole and administered the appropriate antivenom. Although Lib became somewhat woozy and her leg swelled considerably, she survived the encounter. The wound became necrotic and took two to three weeks to heal. There were no long-term consequences. It did teach me a good lesson—not to be cavalier about snakes.

The only other pointer to suffer seriously from a snakebite was a puppy named Charity, a littermate of Faith. At the age of about six months, they were allowed to run around and hunt near the house by themselves. In this situation, the poisonous snake was never seen. Charity was bitten in the face and came running to the house. Faith also was apparently bitten but suffered only minor swelling. Charity was treated with the antivenom, but became quite sick and died six hours later.

My grown pointers seem to know that they should avoid snakes. On several occasions, I have seen them point rattlesnakes. Once, while hunting singles in a fairly open field, I heard a soft, slow clicking sound coming from a four-by-four thicket of broomstraw. Hank stiffened and froze ten feet from the source, but rather than assume a traditional point, he slowly and carefully backed away. The rate of the clicking increased, and its cause, at last, dawned on me. I grabbed Hank by the collar and led him to safety. Upon returning, I found two large diamondback rattlesnakes mating. Being otherwise occupied no doubt had caused their failure to rattle characteristically. I felt somewhat disheartened at ending their courtship, but knew it wasn't the first time lovemaking had ended in disaster.

An episode I won't forget happened one day while Hannah trailed a covey of quail, not knowing a large rattlesnake was also stalking the birds. Hannah came upon the creature, gracefully hurdled it, and went on trailing the quail and finally pointing. She paid no attention to the reptile, being 100 percent focused on the job she had been born to do. Not so disengaged, I killed the snake.

The only other fatality from a rattlesnake bite involved a Labrador retriever named Champ. (Champ's exploits as a retriever of snipe have been detailed elsewhere.) However, his retrieving expertise was not limited to snipe or quail, unfortunately. On one occasion, he thought retrieving a five-foot rattlesnake might be great fun. Champ did not survive the multiple bites. I've not seen any of the other flush dogs, Labrador retrievers, springer spaniels, or cocker spaniels being dimwitted enough to retrieve a rattlesnake. In fact, none of them have been bitten while hunting.

One other recent instance involving a rattlesnake and Horatio remains etched in my memory. It was late in the evening, and we were hunting singles. Horatio was covering the ground in front of us, approximately twenty yards away, and coming toward us. Joey was in front of me. Just as Horatio turned back, Joey shot right over his head. It took me a second or two to realize that Joey wasn't shooting at a bird. A large rattlesnake, absent its head, lay dead in front of us. Joey had made the best shot of his life. I don't think Horatio was aware of the snake; I certainly wasn't. He was headed directly toward disaster, and would have been bitten on the head. I am certain that the pellets passed no more than three inches above Horatio's head.

I carry several vials of the antivenom (approximately $600 a vial) in the truck. This is effective in suppressing the immediate lethal effects of a bite and reducing the subsequent necrosis in the wound. In the past two years, a vaccine to immunize dogs against rattlesnake bites has been developed for the western diamondback rattlesnake. Whether there is a degree of cross-reactivity with the eastern diamondback rattlesnake, at least as best as I can find out, has not been determined. However, all of my dogs have all been immunized.

I continue to hunt in "snake country" and have an encounter with a poisonous snake approximately every two to three years. So far, I have been very lucky. Joey wears snake boots; I do not. I can't walk in them. I have tried snake boots, snake leggings, snake puttees, snake pants, snake chaps—everything. Unfortunately, at least for me, they all are too cumbersome. I do, however, wear a "snake charm." (The type is a secret.) I do hope that I will continue to be lucky regarding poisonous snakes.

At least at this juncture, I rate snake problems as a nuisance, but by no means a reason not to hunt.

Bird Dog Dogma

Chapter XXIX

This particular treatise deals with the dogma involved in praising and admonishing your pointer along with additional complications that arise when accompanied by another hunter, either with or without his bird dog.

An important component of the mystique of bird hunting is to develop a strategy for proudly proclaiming your pointer's peerless performance, or conversely, muttering madly about his misdeeds or malfeasance. When hunting alone, praising the dog and voicing your canine companion's name, followed by a trite phrase such as "good dog," will suffice. To show your disenchantment, using a similar approach while exclaiming, "you son-of-a-bitch," also works reasonably well. (Depending on the situation, additional corrective action may be indicated.) The simplicity of this unfettered technique is a very strong reason to hunt by one's self.

Although not my choice, many reasonably dedicated bird hunters, Havilah Babcock being one of them, opined that bird hunting is at its best when two compatible partners partake in the sport. Let us explore the consequences of critiquing your pointer's performance resulting from this dual approach. If the partner has hunted with you before and does not have a bird dog, the situation becomes only slightly more complicated.

Although it is still reasonable to praise your pointer, you should keep a low profile. Never brag on your pointer until the hunt is over. He may perform perfectly up until the time you start extolling his virtues. However, from that point on, he will point sparrows, flush coveys, run deer, and have an altercation with a skunk. (Pointers have an uncanny ability to make a liar out of you.) Only when the hunt is terminated and everything has gone well should you even suggest that your dog performed well. If your companion brags about your pointer's performance, smile knowingly and agree. Corrective procedures that you deem necessary are not adversely affected by the presence of a compatible hunting companion.

If your companion is accompanied by a bird dog whose abilities are unknown to you, the situation becomes somewhat more involved, but usually is entirely manageable. Remember that quail hunting is a gentleman's sport; conduct yourself in a gentlemanly manner. It is perfectly acceptable to brag on the other man's dog. In fact, even carrying your praise to the unctuous level usually will be appreciated. However never make any disparaging remarks about his dog or even worse, correct the misdeeds. It would be far better to opine that your partner's mother runs a bawdy house, or receives stolen goods, than to intrude into the forbidden "no man's land" of adversely judging or correcting your companion's bird dog. Clearly, if the two of you have hunted together on previous occasions, it is likely that these issues already have been satisfactorily sorted out.

The next step toward potential serious problems, and it's a big one, is to hunt with a heretofore unknown individual. Hunting with a stranger who does not have a bird dog may or may not make you alter the approach to dealing with your dog. Both praise and corrections should be attempted in a manner similar to those previously described.

Dealing with issues other than your bird dog's performance is far more germane to this situation. For example, you must make a quick judgment and act accordingly as to your companion's bird-hunting expertise—always being aware that there is a good chance that either you or your pointer may be shot. Thus, evaluating your bird dog's performance becomes of secondary significance. Only if the individual takes it upon himself to point out every minor or even major misadventure by your dog do you need to be concerned. By far, the best strategy in this situation is to remember the gentleman's code and keep quiet. Perhaps taking the batteries out of your hearing devices so that they function as earplugs will facilitate your serene attitude.

Obviously, if his disenchantment with your pointer progresses to the point of attempted physical correction will you need to intervene. Trying to maintain your composure is best done by using one of the two following strategies. 1) Feign turning your ankle, thereby having to end the hunt. (This is the preferred approach.) 2) If you feel compelled to break the gentlemanly silent approach, indicate that he is exhibiting all of the qualities of a TIP (Total Ignoramus about Pointers). Obviously, following this altercation, you and your pointer will need, like Elvis, to "leave the building."

Now comes the rub. All of the foregoing present only minor difficulties when compared to hunting with a stranger who brings along his dog, usually one of the fuzzy varieties having unknown qualities. Hunting with a stranger should be undertaken for only one reason: The individual has access to the land and the quail, and if he and his dog do not come along, there won't be a hunt. If you agree to participate in this type of exercise, be forewarned that you are likely to be in for a series of trials that will make Job's predicaments seem like eating a piece of chocolate cake.

The first situation that probably will occur is that your hunting companion continually extols the virtues of his dog. In the unlikely event that his dog is performing reasonably well, agree with him. It won't hurt. However, this approach becomes especially trying when his mutt is a disaster. For example, the dog shows no interest whatever in backing and, thus, will always be the front dog on point—if he doesn't run up the birds. When your new "comrade" brags that his dog is finding all the quail, it takes a great deal of restraint to keep one's mouth shut.

However, to salvage any enjoyment from the hunt, my advice is to remain silent. This includes overlooking other misadventures by his canine catastrophe such as carrying off dead birds and either eating or burying them. Also, your colleague may offer ridiculous excuses for his dog's unacceptable behavior. For example, if his mutt immediately runs off and hides under a bush when a shotgun is fired, this action might be excused because of a traumatic occurrence with a firecracker as a puppy. I could go on *ad infinitum*, but the message is the same: Regardless of the infractions by his bird dog, try to be taciturn. Pointing out the obvious faults in a worthless dog will only engender a personal and lifelong animosity.

Although passively accepting the problems in a bad situation is good advice, sometimes it is essentially impossible to follow. Probably, my most trying episode in this regard occurred several years ago when my small female drop, Belle, and I went hunting with a stranger who was deemed to be a bird hunter. He brought along a "professionally trained" Brittany spaniel. This French freak did little except run around and bark at everything until Belle pointed. Instead of backing, he decided it would be an opportune time to try his hand at breeding. Belle was a patient little lady, but after a minute or so of his amorous approach, she broke off point and bit the little bastard. His owner became incensed and started to admonish Belle. At this juncture, I evoked the

"Popeye rule": I've stoods me enough, I can't stands me no more. I called off the hunt, and interdicted further excursions with this pair.

I'm not even going to comment on the issues that arise when hunting with more than one other individual or bird dog. By definition, quail hunting demands the presence of a maximum of two hunters and two bird dogs. Only a seriously deranged individual would be involved with breaking this inviolate rule.

Yes, hunting with a stranger and his bird dog can, and usually does, present a series of difficult problems. After spending the day restraining one's self from commenting, be introspective and ask, "Was it worth the effort?" My guess is that the answer will not be in the affirmative. You can plan appropriately to avoid future hunting excursions with the pair. On the other hand, if you cannot restrain yourself, the time has come to inform the individual that he has a worthless piece of crap for a bird dog and, by inference, owning such a disaster makes him of questionable value as well.

What's the bottom line of all these machinations? At least for me, by far the best approach is to have only one companion in the field—your own bird dog.

Disappearing Dogs

Chapter XXX

One of the primary characteristics of pointers is their aggressive approach to hunting. By that, I mean, they run like hell. Personally, I have always appreciated this characteristic. It is far easier to curtail wide-ranging activities than to cajole a complacent and disinterested dog into hunting rather than being underfoot all the time.

I recognize that many outdoor aficionados, enamored by fuzzy bird dogs, like the companionship of having their dog walk in lock step with them and cover approximately an acre every hour. Since these hunters define this *modus operandi* as the correct way to hunt bird, they invariably describe a pointer as being "out of control" and throw pounds of vitriol on these peerless performers. For example, pointers are knighted as "advertising dogs" i.e., release a pointer and then spend the next week advertising for him in the local papers. This only begins to "scratch the surface" of the invective heaped on pointers, but you get the message.

To be fair, even those that are well trained occasionally absent themselves from view for a while. Usually, the subsequent search ends in finding the dog staunchly on point. In my long-term experience, I have never had to leave a pointer in the field overnight. Hence, pointers disappearing for days have not been a problem for me. On the other hand, from first-hand experience, I do know the concern and agony visited upon one's self by a lost dog. Let me explain.

During the three- to four-year period that I fox hunted, I became thoroughly indoctrinated regarding the misery engendered by a lost dog. In essence, the type of fox hunting that I participated in was to turn a pack of hounds out sometime after dark in an area known to be frequented by foxes. If everything went well, the hounds would jump a fox and run it for several hours while serenading the countryside. When the fox got tired of the "fun" and went into a den, the pack would return to the point where they had been released, usually just after daylight. This describes what is supposed to happen.

However, not infrequently, the dogs would become scattered and sometimes be several miles from where they had been released. One of the characteristics of a good fox hound, in fact, nearly on par with being able to run a fox, is to return to the point of release in a timely manner. A good "homer" is highly prized. Although most of the time retrieving the pack the next day was not too difficult, on more than a few occasions, I spent a considerable amount of time and effort locating a wayward hound.

I learned that three days was a long time to be gone; over a week the dog was unlikely to return. A dog lost for a few days invariably gave the appearance of being on the "last legs" of starvation. In fact, the time spent searching for a missing dog, along with the ever-present concern that the dog was either stolen, hurt, or dead, weighed positively on my decision not to continue with this endeavor.

Toward the end of my fox-hunting career, the lost-dog situation was escalated markedly by the explosive increase in the number of unprincipled deer hunters eager to steal hounds to run deer. Primarily, for this reason, I decided to concentrate on bird hunting. Fox hunting did, in fact, indoctrinate me into the emotional strain of losing a dog.

The primary purpose of this brief communication is to describe my recent travails when my prized pointer escaped from the pen and left the environs. Over the years, I have experienced only a few instances when a pointer absented himself from the pen. Other than leaving the gate open by mistake, a dog escapes either through digging under the fence or going over the top. Many years ago, when I had beagles, I learned that it was quite easy to prevent them from digging under the fence by burying a two-foot section of wire at a right angle to the base of the fence. This technique obviates the dogs from digging out—at least the ones that I have housed. In order to prevent their climbing out, I installed an insulated wire around the top of the pen and connected it to a standard stock fence charger. This technique has been highly successful, except in the following situation.

I recently acquired Bard, an outstanding Elhew-bred pointer. From the moment I first saw him in the field, he "suited me to a T." In Florida, he was housed in a single dog run enclosed by a fence of woven wire six feet tall with the top covered. There was an eighteen-inch opening at the top of the fence. Approximately thirty other pointers are housed in similar pens and not one had escaped previously. When hunted daily, Bard presented no problem. However, on two occasions after a week layover, he decided to go hunting on his own and somehow managed to climb the fence and squeeze through the opening. This portal was closed, and Bard remained in the pen for the rest of the season.

Like many well-heeled citizens, my pointers make an annual pilgrimage from Florida to North Carolina to spend the summer following the end of the quail season. I placed Bard in a pen enclosed by six-foot woven wire with the aforementioned electric wire around the top. Since I had never had a dog escape from this pen, I didn't worry at all. I should have. Three weeks after he arrived, I went to the pen on a Monday morning to feed. Bard was gone. I checked the electrified wire and it was on. On several occasions, I have had dogs get out because the gate was left unlatched, but within an hour or so they always returned. Therefore, I didn't worry too much about Bard at the time. He wore a reasonably tight-fitting nylon collar stamped with all of the pertinent contact information.

I rode around looking for him, fully expecting him to show up that afternoon—no Bard. By the next morning, I started worrying and contacted a number of people who lived within a mile or so of my dog pen and alerted them to this situation. I also called the local animal shelters. A number of my friends and I began to "ride the roads" looking for Bard. In fact, we scoured the area thoroughly, carefully examining both sides of the roads and stopping frequently to shout his name (muttering "son-of-a-bitch" under our breath).

On several occasions, especially late in the evening, I misidentified lawn furniture or garbage cans as Bard. On day four, a physician/neighbor called me to say that he "thought" he had my dog. Unfortunately, this critter was an unidentifiable mutt. To make a long story short, a hell of a search was put on for Bard but to no avail.

After five days with Bard still absent, I began to get really depressed. He had escaped into a several-thousand-acre forest, inhabited by coyotes. In addition, there was a highway approximately one-half mile from the dog pen. I ran a "lost dog" ad offering a reward in the newspaper and continued every day to ride the local roads looking for the escapee. By the end of ten days, I assumed that Bard had been either killed by a vehicle but his body had not been found, killed by coyotes, or that he had been picked up by someone who was not interested in returning him to me, in other words, stolen. I became very despondent, to say the least.

On day thirteen, I got a call from an animal shelter approximately fifteen miles from the dog pen. They had my dog. I dropped what I was doing and hustled over. There was Bard—fit as a fiddle, but without a collar. No. He didn't look like an emaciated dog that had been out on his own for thirteen days. As a matter of fact, he was in top-notch shape, having even gained weight.

It seems that he had been taken to the animal shelter that day by a lady who lived within three-quarters of a mile of my dog pen in a two million dollar mansion. About the time I returned home, this lady called me to say that Bard had been at her house for eleven days. He had appeared in a "starved condition." She had taken him to a veterinarian who had nursed him back to health. She didn't mention, nor did I ask, about the collar. At any rate, in a tear-filled conversation, she indicated that she was very enamored with Bard and would like to buy him. I explained to her that he wasn't really an ideal house pet. I thanked her profusely.

The next day, I sent her a picture of Bard pointing quail, along with the money that she expended on veterinarian bills. (I covered the top of the pen with wire; Bard remained at home for the rest of the summer.) It is unclear exactly why it took her so long to notify me or what happened to the collar. I didn't delve into the matter further. I was happy to have my dog back at home.

One final note. In a couple of days, I received a letter from the lady indicating that she had donated the money I sent to the Humane Society. This was clearly the "unkindness cut of all." My hard-earned money was being used to support that group of antihunting misanthropes!

At any rate, Bard's prolonged disappearing act reinforces my long-term experience: You never know what to expect from a pointer bird dog. On the positive side, Bard had the good sense to take up temporary residence with a very rich woman.

Bird Dogs Who Owned Me

Chapter XXXI

The following briefly lists a number of pointers, a drop, and one setter with which I hunted at least two seasons and consider to be very superior meat dogs. If registered (American Field Dog Stud Book), either the best–known sire or bloodline in the first three generations of the sire are listed followed by similar data for the dam. If either the sire or dam appears on this list, their name is used to designate the breeding. If the breeding is not given, the dog was not registered.

The designation Missy/Missy for Lou requires an explanation. She is a product of a brother/sister mating; thus, her only grandmother is Missy. Lou's son Luke is even more inbred: His sire is also a Missy product. As Joey aptly characterized this breeding: "Luke's family tree doesn't fork."

For the dogs I obtained as an adult, the dates indicate the time period that I hunted with the dog. For the dogs I bred, the initial date listed is the date of birth.

This list does not include the countless numbers of dogs that I have hunted with, albeit briefly, and for various reasons have found wanting. Such a listing would bring back too many unpleasant memories, as well as making it clear that I have expended an enormous amount of money and time on mediocre performers.

Spot
Liver and White
1951–1963

Don
Black and White
1953–1956

Judge
Orange and White
1958–1964

Belle
Black and White
(Drop)
1959–1968

Mack
Liver and White
1962–1972

Cricket
Liver and White
(Luminary/Fast Delivery)
1970–1974

Rena*
Liver and White
(Fast Delivery/Fast Delivery)
1971–1980

Sandy
Liver and White
1975–1982

Gypsy
Liver and White
1978–1985

Pepper
Black and White
(English Setter)
1980–1988

Tiny
Lemon and White
(Carolina Pride/Fast Delivery)
1982–1991

Hannah
Liver and White
(Riggin's White Knight/Red Walter Rex)
1986–1997

*An asterisk indicates the dog is from a litter that I bred.

The following dogs have hunted quail primarily in Florida:

Lib
Liver and White
(Elhew/Pork Roll)
1987–1989

Anne
Liver and White
(Elhew/Lib)
1988–1994

Bonnie
Liver and White
(Elhew/Lib)
1988–1996

Lib II
Liver and White
(Elhew/Lib)
1988–2000

Hank
Black and While
(Guard Rail/Elhew)
1989–1996

Luke*
Black and White
(Hank/Lib II)
1991–2000

Faith*
Black and White
(Hank/Lib II)
1991 – 2005

Sugar
Black and White
(Evolution/Elhew)
1994–2001

Cody
Liver and White
(Guard Rail/Pork Roll)
1995–2001

Missy
Black and White
(Whippoorwill's Rebel/Highway)
1995–2003

Hamlet*
Black and White
(Cody/Missy)
1996–2000

Horatio*
Liver and White
(Cody/Missy)
1996–

Humphrey*
Black and White
(Cody/Missy)
1996–2008

Lou
Black and White
(Missy/Missy)
2000–

Luke* (The Younger)
Black and White
(Missy/Lou)
2001–

Jeb
Lemon and White
(Silverwood/Evolution)
2002–2007

Ulysses*
Black and White
(Jeb/Lou)
2005–

Scylla*
Black and White
(Jeb/Lou)
2005 –

Tyre*
Black and White
(Jeb/Lou)
2006–

Virgo*
Liver and White
(Jeb/Hamlet)
2006–

Bard
Lemon and White
(Elhew/Elhew)
2007–

Pepper
Liver and White
(Honky Tonk Attitude/
Guard Rail)
2007–

Reflections

Chapter XXXII

A broad panorama of my experiences quail hunting for more than sixty years, along with specific aspects of this sport, have been detailed in the preceding chapters. Obviously, during this period, I traveled from adolescence to "old" age with the resultant alterations in my life. Now, I would like to focus on what hunting bobwhite quail has meant to me during this journey. How have I been affected? Am I smarter, richer, or better looking because of this extended experience?

The choice of the word "odyssey" to characterize my bird-hunting adventures is somewhat misleading. In Homer's classic, throughout his ten years of wandering, Ulysses sought to go home and be reunited with Penelope. In spite of the fact that he had to kill Penelope's multiple suitors, the end of his odyssey was a welcome event. On the other hand, my six-decade pursuit of bobwhite quail has only whetted my appetite for more. Even now, when I close my eyes, my first covey rise becomes a reality. This tableau has not been dimmed, but instead has been brilliantly illuminated by the many thousands of subsequent explosive bevies. Although unrealistic, I hope that my odyssey never ends!

During the past twenty-five years, I have been affected profoundly by my close friendship with Joey O'Bannon. Joey has given me the opportunity to continue to explore my passion for quail hunting as well as functioning as a unique hunting companion. In fact, Joey is the only individual with whom I have had an extended quail-hunting partnership, for as you know by now, I have always preferred hunting quail by myself. Another major factor in my life due to Joey has been my recent experiences hunting dangerous game in Africa. Without his encouragement, these challenges would never have taken place.

For me, 1996 was a major milestone. Upon stepping down as chairman of the Department of Medicine at Duke University Medical Center, I had to decide, what's next? Further administrative activities had no appeal whatsoever. (I hate meetings, especially the proforma type with people I dislike.) In similar situations, many of my colleagues have become involved with a variety of "think tank" opportunities—the general gist of which is formulating plans to tell other physicians how to live their lives (not an interest of mine). Another group has carried out research, either clinical or basic. I had done both and decided that I had little creativity left to offer in either arena.

Many have chosen to obtain advanced degrees to prepare them for future activities. For me, this plan seemed to have a great deal of promise. Rather than obtaining a M.P.H. or M.B.A., I chose to confine my labors to the M.M.B.A.—Miles and Miles of Bloody Africa. At this writing, I have completed twelve safaris (seven of which were chronicled in *Bwana Babu)*, and taken the African Big Five. I am certain that this exercise would neither be sought by nor be suitable for many people, but for me it has been ideal. Besides the excitement of hunting dangerous game, these experiences have allowed me to contemplate my place in the greater scheme of reality as well as my own fragile mortality.

To return to the pursuit of bobwhite quail, I am a dyed-in-the-wool, dedicated bird hunter. As detailed elsewhere, this sport can be considered to consist of three different, but interrelated, components: bird dogs, killing quail, and shotguns. Although I am interested in the latter two, clearly my admiration and love for pointer bird dogs has kept me looking forward to every experience with them. Interacting with my dogs on a daily basis and being involved in their care, feeding, and training has been richly rewarding. As a group, pointers care for little else than hunting. Thus, the close bonding relationship that most dog lovers require does not occur. This doesn't bother me. I have learned to admire the single-purpose goal that pointers have in life. In fact, I have learned an important lesson: If you want to be successful, concentrate on one thing and do it well.

Initially, my training efforts were almost exclusively with at least partially trained pointers that needed only to be hunted to complete their skills. However, in the last two decades of my odyssey, I have begun breeding and carrying out the initial training for a number of pointer puppies. I have learned a great deal not only about handling different personalities but also about how to identify outstanding prospects (not that I have become an expert in this endeavor other than to estimate the key factors of intelligence and smelling ability).

However, having the opportunity to mold the development of young pointers, besides being fun, has been of immeasurable value in helping me to train physicians more effectively. Follow the maxim: Be certain that the pupils understand the appropriate goals and then get out of the way and let them develop. To watch either a bird dog puppy or a young physician suddenly realize what he is suppose to do, as though a light went on in his head, is a very fulfilling experience.

In order to kill quail, they first must be located. Obviously, the pointers carry the lion's share of the work in this regard. On the other hand, the expertise of the hunter regarding where and when to find quail will contribute, at least to some extent, in the success of the hunt. I have made a lifelong, in-depth study of many of the factors involved in hunting quail, and these include wind direction, scenting conditions, quail movement, cover, and feeding habits—to name a few. Primarily, what I have learned from these endeavors is humility. Just about the time I conclude that I am well versed in the foregoing, I am proven wrong. Learning to be humble is a hard, but vital, lesson.

Concentrating on the task at hand is an essential feature in the killing of quail. Here my performance is sub-par, primarily dictated by the fact that I am so enamored with watching the bird dogs that shooting in a timely fashion takes a back burner. I have not, nor ever will I learn to approach the pointed dog with the single purpose in mind of killing quail. (Luckily, most of my pointers are tolerant of my poor marksmanship.) The lesson I have gained is that it is not necessary to excel in every aspect of a sport to thoroughly enjoy participating.

In the initial years of my odyssey, I became extraordinarily enamored with collecting double-barrel shotguns, specifically Parkers. In fact, at one time I had an example of every grade of 12-gauge shotgun that Parker made in my gun safe. One day, while engaged in a semi-annual cleaning chore, it occurred to me that the adage "He who dies with the most toys wins" is a very shallow goal. I thought the situation through and arrived at the conclusion that winning a "gun collection accolade" was not a reasonable achievement for me. Accordingly, over a ten-year period, I sold the collection and used the proceeds to further my hunting adventures. Except for the side-by-side, double-barrel shotguns that I use to hunt on a regular basis, my gun safe is quite bare. Frankly, I'm very happy with the trade off of guns for fun.

To sum up: No, I am not smarter (maybe wiser), richer (far from it), or better looking (only wrinkled) as a result of my more than six-decade, quail-hunting odyssey. As highlighted in the following poem, myriad magical memories forever are etched in my being. Like a child unable to sleep, waiting for the marvels of Christmas morning, I eagerly await the next episode in my quail-hunting odyssey.

To Be Remembered

As man struggles through his daily test,
A few memories rise above the rest—
Closely cherished as special to him,
To be remembered when all else grows dim.
The ruby fire in a gamecock's eye as he's pitted to fight;
The music that floats from a foxhound pack on a clear October night;

The feel of a Purdey shotgun shouldered to fire;
Pointers running "big" with speed, style and desire,
Pointing in a dreamlike trance, rigid as a stone;
The whirling thunder a covey makes leaving for parts unknown.
Yes, these are the memories I'll hold close,
When I answer the call from the Heavenly Host.
(1995)

Glossary

This book contains considerable jargon that, though familiar to bird hunters, may be opaque to the uninitiated. The following attempts to clarify some of this terminology.

Back: Refers to the brace mate of the dog pointing. The brace mate must stop and point as soon as the pointing dog is seen. Most pointers hate to back because they usually cannot smell the birds. They'll try a number of tricks—especially feigning temporary blindness—to shirk this duty.

Bird: In the vernacular of Southern hunters, bird means quail. The words "quail" and "bird" are used interchangeably in the text. Quail were identified as "pottages" by sharecropper farmers.

Bird-Shy or Blinker: When bird scent is perceived, the dog runs away, rather than points—a major fault caused by excessive punishment. The best recourse is to sell a bird-shy dog to an enemy.

Bird Sense: A pointer's ability, gained through breeding and experience, to find and handle quail.

Bolt: A pointer that when released leaves the environs post haste and returns, if ever, several hours later thoroughly exhausted. A confirmed bolter is essentially worthless.

Bottom: This term has nothing to do with the dog's rear-end. It is used to describe the dog's staying power or endurance.

Broke: Although this word usually carries a negative connotation (without money or shattered glass), in this context it defines a well-trained pointer.

Drop: A crossbreed that is half pointer/half setter; generally, a mediocre bird dog. The superior qualities of the pointer can't overcome the setter's negative features.

Flagging / Ticking: While pointing, the tail is moved from side to side; thereby, markedly detracting from the intensity of the style.

Force-Broken to Retrieve: Training pointers to retrieve by relying on natural instincts won't work; they have none. The pointer must learn to retrieve, like it or not; hence, the term "force- broken."

Gun Shy: A dog that clears out for parts unknown when a gun is fired; this fault is difficult, but not impossible, to correct.

Meat Dog: Although this pointer may exhibit less than high-quality style, he is a reliable bird dog. If there are birds around, he will find them.

Over-broke: A dog that is too cautious, shows little style, and has a tendency to cower; caused by excessive punishment during training and usually isn't remedial.

Pointer, English Pointer: The word pointer describes a specific breed; thus, the designation "English" is superfluous. However, English pointer is frequently used in this text, lest the reader think the discussion involves German shorthair pointers, a most sub-optimal breed.

Potter: The dog repeatedly trails over the same unproductive old scent while the birds are elsewhere. A pottering dog should be culled.

Range: The pattern or distance a pointer runs from the hunter. The range of a pointer is classified as close (under foot all the time) or wide (hunting in the next county).

Started: Should define a pointer showing progress in initial training. Buying a "started dog" usually means that the animal has no training whatever or is too dense to learn.

Staunch: A pointing dog that will not move until ordered to relocate—an essential trait. When carried to an extreme, the dog may be left behind by running birds.

Stink Bird: Any species of small bird, such as a field sparrow, whose scent may be mistaken for quail by a pointer.

Stop to Flush: When a bird is inadvertently flushed, the pointer stops, as if to say, "Sorry for the mistake."

Style/Class: Denotes the appearance of a pointer both while hunting and pointing and includes intensity, enthusiasm, and, in my view, beauty. The concept is hard to define precisely. If the pointing dog gives the impression he has stopped to empty his bladder—that ain't style.

Trash: Any critter that distracts a pointer e.g., dove, snipe, box turtles, rabbits, hogs, or deer.

Bibliography

Babcock, Havilah. *My Health is Better in November.* New York: Holt, Reinhart and Winston, 1947.

——. *I Don't Want to Shoot an Elephant.* New York: Holt, Rinehart and Winston, 1958.

——. *Jaybirds Go to Hell on Friday.* New York: Holt, Rinehart, and Winston, 1965.

Buckingham, Nash. *Mark Right.* New York: Derrydale Press Inc., 1936.

Greenfield, Joseph C., Jr. *Bwana Babu.* Long Beach: Safari Press, 2005

Pollard, Hugh B.C. *The Mystery of Scent.* London: Eyre and Spottiswoode, 1937.

Stoddard, Herbert L. *The Bob White Quail, Its Habits, Preservation and Increase,* New York: Charles Scribner's Sons, 1931.